THE ART OF RETIREMENT FOR WOMEN

7 Simple Steps to Overcome Uncertainty, Cultivate Passion, Spark Joy, and Find Fulfillment

BARBARA J. DE EDUARDO

COPYRIGHT & TRADEMARKS

the information contained within this document, including, but not limited to, — errors, omissions, or inaccuracies.

<u>Trademarks:</u> All trademarks, trade names, or logos mentioned or used are the property of their respective owners. Every effort has been made to properly capitalize, punctuate, identify and attribute trademarks and trade names to their respective owners, including the use of ® and ™ wherever possible and practical. All trademarks are the property of their respective owners.

Dedication

To my beautiful wife and partner in life, L.P.
Your love, encouragement and laughter inspire me to explore the uncertainty of life with
excitement, hope and confidence.
I would not be the woman I am without you.
I love you to the moon and back.

***

To the women in my life, like my mother, who paved the way, who dared to break the mold,
who rewrote the rules, and lived life on their own terms.
This book is for the dreamers, the doers, the late bloomers, and the never-settlers.
May your retirement be a time of discovery, joy, and unapologetic adventure.
And to those still searching for their "one thing"
I dedicate this to the courage it takes to start again, no matter the age or stage.

Here's to your encore.
Make it unforgettable!

TABLE OF CONTENTS

PROLOGUE

I never planned to author a book about retirement. Honestly, planning too far in advance has never been my strong suit. I've always just jumped in, feet first, trusting that something interesting would happen along the way. It's what led me to leave a perfectly safe (and soul-sucking) engineering career at IBM to work in technical publishing. Four months into that job, the company shut its doors. Not exactly what I had envisioned. But instead of retreating, I called upon two friends, and together we spun the business into something of our own. The company did well for 22 years, and we were coming to a natural close when the COVID pandemic and lockdown hit speeding things up much faster than I had planned. And — like a newborn chick being prematurely pushed from the nest, I did what any 60-year-old chick would do — I hit rock bottom.

March 17th, the day the lockdown began in California, my sister-in-law passed away after years of battling cancer. It was with hindsight we realized what a gift it was to be able to have family around her while she passed on. Then, less than a month later, my youngest sister died unexpectedly. There was no way for our family to come together and grieve.

My grief was deep and so unresolved it was hard to even breathe. Twinned with the crushing fear of COVID, normal life was transformed into upside down abnormal with breathtaking speed. Life with masks, gloves, hand sanitizers, and unexplainable toilet paper shortages became the new normal. Even the simplest, mundane of things like grocery shopping became more of a strategic deployment, timed for the early morning "Elder Hour" (60+ shoppers only) so it would be a short wait in line — six feet apart — to get in the store because now, only so many shoppers could be inside at the same time.

It was my dark night of the soul. I was angry, depressed, gaining weight, and spiraling into a version of myself I didn't recognize. Retirement? That was the furthest thing from my mind. What I was really doing was figuring out how to get out of bed each morning, in a world literally closed down, without feeling like the walls were closing in.

But then, as life often does, it sent a lifeline — or perhaps you'd call it a miracle. Some might say it was God, the universe, or just fate at work, but there it was: the proverbial boat pulling up alongside me in the form of a Tony Robbins virtual event. Of course, the challenge wasn't just seeing the boat — it was deciding to climb into it. And let me tell you, I didn't exactly leap aboard. My wife, bless her, practically pushed me in by signing me up for his five-day Comeback Challenge. I rolled my eyes so hard I'm surprised they didn't get stuck. I recall not being very happy about it but we were in lock down and honestly, there was nothing better to do. I headed to the spare bedroom, clutching my 'Comeback Challenge' kit — with four emoji placards glued to tongue depressors, a mini notebook with a pen — and, of course, snacks.

The "Comeback Challenge" (ironic chuckle) opened my eyes to something I'd forgotten — I can change how I feel by moving my body. Each day of the Challenge started with high energy music that made it impossible for me not to dance! And I wasn't alone! This virtual event had at least 22,000 people in their homes, on their feet, raising their energy and I could feel it. The energy hit me like a wave and for the first time in a very long time, I felt alive again and full of hope.

One major takeaway, out of many from my "Tony Time", stuck with me — *"Change your state, change your energy, change your life"*. I started to see how music was a powerful tool in shifting my energy. I experienced first hand how a themed playlist of songs changed my energy from unhopeful to downright giddy! Music alone could shift my feeling defeated to ready to take on the world all by cranking up a great song and moving.

Now don't misunderstand, my eye rolls went on for months! Each virtual event I participated in I scoffed at what I thought to be 'woo woo' activities. But like most everything I have ever done in my life, I jumped in with both feet! Somewhere along the way, though, a shift started happening. I couldn't help but think about the big questions these events brought up — questions about purpose, joy, and what really matters in life.

That's when my mind wandered to one of my favorite movies, "*City Slickers*". I have seen it a million times! There's a scene where Curly, played by the iconic Jack Palance as the grizzled cowboy, tells Mitch that the secret to life is just *"one thing."* Using, shall we say, colorful language, Curly explains that the *"one thing"* is all that matters. When Mitch asks, "That's great, but what's the one thing?" Curly responds, "That's what *you* gotta figure out."

Watch the scene on YouTube using the QR code below.

There is so much truth to the wisdom of this movie's theme — figure out what the *"one thing"* is. No one can tell you what *your* thing is. Like Curly says, *"you gotta figure it out."* Each of us needs to find that *"one thing"*, but most of us are at a loss on how to find it. Like many things in life, there is no instruction manual on how to find what makes your heart smile. For me, and quite by accident, I discovered that the music I grew up with was my "hack" for reconnecting with the joy and hope I had in my younger years, before being an adult took over.

> *Let me digress a little here and define what I mean by a "hack" because, when I was growing up the word didn't mean anything good! But in today's culture a "hack" is like a super power and typically its finding smart, often non-traditional ways to solve problems in everyday life.*

Music is my hack, my secret sauce for getting unstuck from the rigid mindset of working for a living. I leverage music as a tool to inspire and motivate myself. Maybe music is your thing too or maybe it's something quite different. Perhaps hiking, traveling, movies, art, cooking, or even gardening. The point is we each have a special key — a can opener if you will — to unlock, explore and create a retirement that is amazing and unique to each of us.

The challenge lies in finding what motivates and excites you. And that is what this book is about — finding that *"one thing"* and leveraging the **hell** out of it to help overcome the preconceived notions about being a 'woman of a certain age' who is about to retire or already retired.

The thing is, no one really prepares you for what retirement feels like. Sure, we all get bombarded with the financial advice (and yes, that's important), but if you're mentally, emotionally, and physically drained, how are you supposed to *enjoy* it? That's why I wrote this book. Because retirement should be a time when you're thriving, not just surviving. It's your time to rediscover who you are, what makes you happy, and how to live with purpose again.

One of the beautiful aspects of retirement is that it is highly personal. No two retirement experiences are the same because no two people are the same. This book provides a road map, but the direction you take is entirely up to you. You will find practical advice and inspiration to help you craft a retirement that reflects your unique passions and interests. Whether it's learning a new language, mastering the art of leisure, or finally writing *your* book, retirement can be a time to follow dreams and set new goals.

So let's get started. This isn't the end — it's your encore. And it's going to be amazing!

CHAPTER ONE

INTRODUCTION: THE ART OF RETIREMENT FOR WOMEN

Retirement is often seen as the final chapter in the book of life — a winding down, a slow fade into the background. But what if it could be something more? What if retirement were not the end of a journey, but something new and exciting? For many women, this stage of life presents a unique opportunity to rediscover themselves, to re-friend passions long set aside, and to live with a renewed sense of purpose and joy. "The Art of Retirement for Women" is a guide to show you options on how to change *surviving retirement* to *thriving in retirement*.

In this book, we'll break away from traditional stereotypes that bellow this time is for rest, relaxation and for fading into the sunset of irrelevance. What we are asking is what does it look like to embrace the idea that retirement is a canvas waiting to be painted with the colors of your choosing? A time to create, to grow, and to enjoy the fullness of life. We'll journey through the essential elements of a fulfilling retirement: from cultivating a healthy lifestyle and nurturing social connections to embracing lifelong learning and finding purpose in everyday routines.

Retirement is not merely the absence of work; it's the presence of freedom — freedom to explore new hobbies, travel to uncharted destinations, and invest time in relationships that truly matter. But with this freedom comes the challenge of redefining who you are outside the roles that have defined you for so long. It's about expanding beyond the titles and embracing the multi-faceted woman you've always been. This book is your companion in a journey of self-discovery, encouraging you to ask, "What do I want to do next?" and "How can I make this the best chapter of my life?"

***

Let's take a moment to appreciate just how much time we've spent working. We spend about 90,000 hours on average at work over our lifetime. Assuming most of us don't sleep on the job, that's roughly one-third of our waking hours! And, let's not forget the commute — 225 hours a year spent just getting to and from work. Over a 45-year career, that's over 10,000 hours on the road. Many of us put in more than the standard 40 hours a week, with half of Americans working overtime and about 18% clocking over 60 hours weekly. It's no wonder that when retirement comes, the silence can feel deafening and frankly, a little disorienting.

Retirement can often feel like a vast, unstructured stretch of time. While this can be freeing, it can also be daunting. How do you fill your days in a way that feels meaningful? This book encourages you to live with intention, to find small daily practices that bring joy and satisfaction, and to cultivate a mindset of mindfulness and gratitude. From developing a purposeful daily routine to creating a living space that feels harmonious and inspiring, you will find practical advice to make every day feel like a new adventure.

What this book doesn't cover is financial strategies — there's plenty of excellent books, YouTube channels and experts out there to guide you on that front. I'm not one of them and neither is this book! "The Art of Retirement for Women" tunes into the emotional, mental, physical, and spiritual well-being challenges that come with retirement. It's a guide with suggestions for reconnecting with your passions, staying active, and engaging with your community — all set to the soundtrack of music, the "Playlist of My Life." From Bon Jovi's "It's My Life" to Tina Turner's "Steamy Windows" to Bruce Springsteen's "Born to Run," these anthems bring back the energy of life memories and inspire new adventures.

"The Art of Retirement for Women" is an invitation to re-imagine what retirement can be without the filters that society wants you to have. It is your choice to see this time ahead not as an inevitable period of decline but as a time of renewal and growth. In these pages, you will find stories from women who have navigated this transition before you — stories of reinvention, of finding new passions, and of creating a retirement that feels rich and rewarding. These narratives are not just inspirational; they are proof that retirement is what you make of it.

This book is structured around 7 Simple Steps, each headlining great music, take aways, and stories from others who have found joy and fulfillment in their retirement years. Whatever your *"one thing"* is — whether it's volunteering at a local charity, joining an adventure group of like-minded women, or discovering (or rediscovering) a hobby — this book invites you to theme your retirement to the music or that *"one thing"* that moves you.

Designed to be inclusive, "The Art of Retirement for Women" welcomes all women and anyone eager to approach retirement as a vibrant stage of life. It's an invitation to explore the rhythms of retirement and discover how to live your best life in this liberating new phase. Whether you are just beginning this journey or are already well into it, this book is here to remind you that retirement is not the end, it's your encore.

So let's grab the bull by the horns and talk about the emotional, spiritual and physical mindset of retiring. While this isn't complex, it's not easy. We all have a lot of peer pressure on who and what we should be. Shedding that takes courage but trust me, it is a worthy effort. So let's embrace it with open arms, an open heart, and a spirit ready to explore the endless possibilities that lie ahead.

Chapter Two

REDISCOVER AND PURSUE YOUR PASSIONS

There were mornings I woke up, half-asleep, still programmed that it was time to face another day at work. I stumbled out of bed, grabbed my coffee, and even started looking for my car keys — like I was late or something. As I stood there, a little confused, it hit me — *I'm retired*! No one is waiting for me at the office, there are no deadlines, no meetings... and definitely no reason to be in such a hurry! I blinked, laughed at myself, and took a deep breath.

I stood there, my to-go coffee in hand, thinking now that I had all this extra time what on earth was I going to do with it. It was like being a kid again, except instead of a summer break, this was *the rest of my life*. It took a few minutes to sink in that every day could be a slow, beautiful morning of "absolutely anything."

***

Let's consider how much time most of us have spent working for a living and do a little math to put it into perspective. Don't worry, this isn't a math quiz!

Starting with recent data for women in developed countries we calculate the following:

- **Average lifespan**: 81 years

- **Average working hours**: 100,000 hours (90,000 hours over a 45-year span, with an additional 10,000 hours commuting)
  Note: this doesn't take into account that almost 20% of women work 60+ hours a week.

- **Calculate retirement years**: Assuming the average retirement age is 65, a woman would have around 16 years of retirement

- **Total retirement hours** - 16 years × 365.25 days per year × 24 hours per day = 140,256 hours in retirement

We spend close to 42% of our life doing possibly everything but what truly ignites our spirits! But we're also are left with a whopping 58% of our life not working! Let's make this easy and say 8% of that time was when we were kids. We still are left with 50% of our life in retirement...not working for a living...pretty much living for a living.

What if we took this time as a personal backstage pass to discover, or rediscover, and pursue those passions that got tucked away in the hustle of career and life? Retirement isn't about killing time; it's about filling your life with the things that make your heart sing. It is my deepest hope that this book offers you inspiration on what makes ***your*** heart sing.

Let's dive in to this chapter of your vibrant encore where we will sync our hearts with our deepest desires and drum up the courage to pursue them. Remember, connecting with your passions isn't a frivolous endeavor. It's a vital pursuit to leading a fulfilling life, especially now, when time is finally on your side. So let's fine-tune our lives to the rhythm of joy and satisfaction.

Here is a QR code to a playlist on Youtube for this book so you can follow along and start formulating what is going to be in your playlist!

"It's My Life": Rediscover Your Playlist of Life

Music is a universal language of mood, emotion, and memory and, as I've mentioned, it provides a fantastic "hack" for our journey into rediscovery. Think about those songs you used to play on repeat, the ones that made you dance or sing into your hairbrush. These aren't just songs, they're time machines capable of whisking you back to moments of absolute joy and vibrant energy. Why not let them inspire you now? And, what better song is there to lead with for our playlist than Bon Jovi's "It's My Life"?

I love learning the backstory about things and was curious about the behind story of this song's lyrics. When asked about it, John Francis Bongiovi, Jr. (aka Bon Jovi) said "I thought I was writing very self-indulgently about my own life and where I was in it. I didn't realize that the phrase "It's My Life" would be taken as being about everyone... It's my life, and I'm taking control."

Zero in on "*self-indulgent*" and understand that if you have never been indulgent with yourself, now is the time to start. It isn't selfish to want a better version of yourself and your life. It doesn't take away from caring about others, it makes you better at it!

Songs we grew up with connect us to the passions in our hearts that have been long forgotten. They can build a bridge from work life to retirement. They can inspire new interests and energize each blessed day we have on this earth. Let them guide you as you turn up the volume on your favorite tracks. Resist filtering your feelings, instead examine them and let your passions lead the way.

Reflective Prompt: Take a moment to think about a time when you felt most alive and passionate. What were you doing? What music was playing? Write down a few activities or hobbies that brought you joy but may have been put on the back burner during your working years.

"Steamy Windows": Rediscover Forgotten Passions

When looking for a beacon of motivation, look no further than Tina Turner. Her incredible career longevity and ability to reinvent herself repeatedly are nothing short of inspirational. Tina's story shows us that age and time don't have to be constraints but can be merely contexts. Her energetic performances and resilience in overcoming personal and professional challenges illustrate the power of passion and perseverance. Her songs are a reminder that it's never too late to revisit an old passion.

Now imagine a room filled with dusty boxes, each one holding memories and dreams you stored away before adult responsibilities took the front seat. Lift the lid on one of these boxes with a sense of adventure. Is it the vinyl record collection that you cherished? Or maybe old journals filled with entries of the thoughts and emotions from your younger self, like frozen moments of time. You kept those mementos for a reason. There is no better time than now to blow the dust off those boxes and embrace the memories contained within. This isn't just a metaphor. It's a call to action. Select what feelings you want to re-experience and bring them forward to this moment in time and let yourself feel the joy of those moments.

But let's be real about sauntering down memory lane — not all your memories will be ones you want to embrace, but they should be ones you learned from. Tina Turner summed it up beautifully.

> Sometimes you've got to let everything go — purge yourself. If you are unhappy with anything...whatever is bringing you down, get rid of it.
> Because you'll find that when you're free, your true creativity, your true self comes out.
>
> Tina Turner

When you let go of baggage that no longer serves your best interest you make room in your life and heart for what does. Engaging with your passions is a statement of self-love and affirmation that the years behind you have wisdom in helping to create the joy in the moments to come.

"Another Brick in the Wall": Break Down the Retirement Stereotypes

It's high time we smash through the gray facade of stereotypes about retirement, like a rock star smashing a guitar on stage. Society has painted retirement as a slow march toward irrelevance for too long. But the truth is, it's anything but. Retirement isn't the final bow. It's the encore everyone's been waiting for, packed with unscripted moments and opportunities for personal reinvention. For women, especially, this period is ripe for rediscovery and shaking up the status quo of what it means to be a retiree.

Think about the rock legends who reinvented themselves time and time again. Retirement offers the same boundless opportunities. It's a chance to shed former roles and explore different facets of your personality and interests. Society often casts a wet blanket over this potential, burdening retirees with droll expectations like "retirement means taking it easy" or "you should focus on your grandchildren", or "it's too late to start something new." These clichés are as outdated as an 8-track tape player. Breaking free from these stereotypes means tuning into your desires and aspirations, not being "just another brick in the wall".

How do we do this? Start small — change the channel. If you've always wanted to start painting — sign up for that art class. If you've dreamt of rock climbing — strap on those harnesses and don't look down. Whenever someone tries to mute your ambitions with their limitations, crank up your personal anthem and remember that retirement is your stage.

Don't be afraid to look to others for inspiration. Rock legend Stevie Nicks, for instance, could have hung up her microphone years ago. She's still electrifying sold out venues of audiences that are generational! She is crushing every stereotype about age and is a testament to the enduring power of following one's passion, regardless of the year on your birth certificate.

If there is only ONE thing you take away from this book, let it be this: the only permission you need to try something new or reinvent yourself, is your own. Embracing your life as a renaissance rather than a retreat requires a mix of defiance and determination. Sculpting a life that reflects your personal aspirations is about picking up the pieces of dreams deferred and building something beautiful with them, not despite your age but because of it. Let your retirement be loud. Let it be less about fitting into a mold and more about breaking the mold apart.

Reflective Prompt: Reflect on the stereotypes or societal expectations you've encountered about retirement. How have these perceptions shaped your view of this phase of life? What new perspectives or beliefs would you like to adopt? Write down how you plan to redefine your own retirement narrative.

"Start Me Up": Kickstart Your Retirement Journey

Now, what tunes will headline your show? What songs get your feet tapping or makes you search for your hairbrush? Discovering these anthems is a deeply personal process and it's much more than nostalgia; they're a reservoir of emotional energy that can inspire and motivate you. But don't stop at the past. Part of the fun is exploring new genres and artists. Who knows? Your new favorite anthem might be waiting in a playlist you've never imagined exploring.

Once you've started identifying these tracks, it's time to organize them purposefully. Creating thematic playlists is a fantastic way to keep your musical needs organized and ready to amplify whatever mood or activity you're diving into. For instance, a 'Chill Morning Coffee' playlist could feature mellow tracks like Norah Jones or Jack Johnson, while a 'Getting Things Done' playlist might be full of energetic hits from BTO, Garth Brooks or Heart.

Leveraging music to lift yourself is not new age mumbo jumbo. The therapeutic benefits of music are well-documented. Recent studies show music's ability to reduce stress, improve mood, and enhance cognitive functioning. By aligning your playlists with your activities or moods, you effectively harness these benefits, making each day a little brighter and bolder.

Expanding your musical horizons is also key. While it's comforting to stick to the old classics, a world of music is out there waiting to be discovered. Every era, every genre has its gems and thanks to modern technology accessing these treasures is easier than ever. And here's the kicker — using music streaming services like Amazon Music, Spotify or Apple Music, can be absolutely free or done at a low monthly subscription fee. These platforms are not just libraries of almost every song you can think of, but also powerful tools for discovering new music and managing your collections.

Here's a quick guide on getting the most out of these services: sign up for an account. Amazon Music, Spotify, and Apple Music offer free trials so you can explore without commitment. Once you're in, search for your favorite songs and artists. As you listen, these platforms will begin to understand your tastes and offer personalized recommenda-tions. This feature is like having a radio station that only plays tracks you're likely to enjoy. Remember to explore the curated playlists and radio stations. They are often grouped by mood, activity, or even time of day, which can be perfect when you're looking for something new but unsure where to start.

Creating your own playlists on these platforms is straightforward. On Spotify, for exam-ple, simply click 'New Playlist,' give it a name that resonates with you and start adding songs. You can create as many playlists as you like — perhaps one for every mood or activity that fills your days. Find a new artist or album that catches your ear? You can save it to your library with just a click, ensuring your musical landscape is always fresh and engaging.

Remember, retirement is about filling your time with joy and meaning. Music can be a powerful companion on this adventure with its profound capacity to touch our hearts and lift our spirits. So, turn up the volume on those songs that inspire you and let the rhythm of your favorite tunes propel you into this exciting phase of life. Every day presents a new opportunity to queue up your crafted playlist and play it loud.

"Go Your Own Way": Craft a Personal Retirement Path

The importance of forging a retirement path reflecting your individuality cannot be overstated. It's embracing who you are and what you love without reservation. For instance, while many might enjoy tending to a garden or playing golf, you might feel more aligned with writing poetry, backpacking through Asia, or even taking an afternoon nap. Listening to that inner voice is essential. This is your time to explore your interests and follow your own beat in a world that too often moves to the rhythm of conformity.

Avoiding the comparison trap is crucial in this journey. With platforms like Facebook and Instagram showcasing highlight reels of lives in perpetual glamour, it's easy to feel your retirement should look a certain way. But here's a little secret, those feeds are not the entire picture of anyone's life, they're just the highlights of the highlight moments. Comparing your every day to someone else's social media persona is a dangerous and unrealistic standard that can steal the joy from your unique retirement experiences. Instead, celebrate that your retirement doesn't look like anyone else's and is as unique as you — perhaps a little eclectic, but, surprising, and deeply satisfying.

Embracing new paths and opportunities in retirement should feel authentically yours, one delightful day at a time. So, whether it's taking a painting class that challenges your creative limits, playing pickle ball or crocheting a blanket for your new grandchild, each new experience is a step towards a more fulfilled and joyful retirement. These experiences not only broaden your horizons but also provide beautiful stories to share. Just like the music you listen to, it resonates and inspires long after the last note has played.

Take Away

For a moment, let's pause the music and reflect on the essence of what we've explored. We've tuned into how music can amplify the joy of reengaging with our passions and how it can be a beacon guiding us through the fog of societal expectations about retirement. We've learned from the legends of rock that reinventing is the mother of necessity and discovered the importance of personalizing our retirement path, ensuring it harmonizes perfectly with who we are and aspire to be. Now, it's time to put these insights into practice and move from being a spectator to taking the stage.

Activity: Create Your Life's Playlist

Let's dive into a fun, engaging activity designed to reflect on this chapter's insights and act on them. I invite you to create "Your Life's Playlist." This isn't just any playlist. It's a collection of songs that define different aspects of your life and aspirations for your retirement.

Reflective Prompt: Spend some time thinking about the various phases of your life — young adulthood, midlife and retirement. What songs come to mind when you think about these times? Which tunes sparked joy, offered comfort, or motivated you during challenges? Write these down.

Organize: Organize these songs into categories based on the feelings from your memories and create a playlist named to remind you what the feeling is when you listen. For example, I have a playlist titled "MovUA$$" filled with high energy songs that I listen to when I workout. It inspires and encourages me to move, and frankly, the title just makes me smile!

Explore: Now, expand your playlist by exploring new music. Dive into different genres or artists you've never considered before. Add a few songs to your playlist that resonate with your current interests and aspirations. Maybe a new jazz album reflects your newfound interest in painting or a classic rock song embodies your desire to travel more.

Use it: Finally, make a point to listen to one or more, of your playlists daily. Play it when you're going about your day, whether gardening, cooking, writing, or just having a cup of coffee. Let each song remind you of your growth and future aspirations.

As you play with this activity, remember the key is to enjoy the process. There's no right or wrong way to create Your Life's Playlist. It's a personal and creative expression of who you are and who you want to be. It's about tuning into what resonates with you and adjusting the volume on the areas of life that matter most to you. Play it loud, sing along, and maybe even dance a little. After all, this is your life, your music, your retirement. Make it count, make it memorable, and most importantly, make it yours.

CHAPTER THREE

EMBRACE A HEALTHY LIFESTYLE

As we dive into this chapter, let's chat about something close to our hearts — our health. Retirement is the perfect time to focus on ourselves and embracing a healthy lifestyle can make these years truly shine. We're not talking about drastic changes or giving up all the fun stuff, but finding a balance that makes us feel our best. Maybe it's a daily walk, trying out The Mediterranean Diet, or simply eating a bit more greens — every little bit counts.

Just as a vibrant live show thrives on energy and enthusiasm, your well-being in retirement flourishes with a bit of physical and mental exercise. Think of this chapter as your backstage pass to the healthiest, most energetic version of yourself. It's more than adding years to your life, but life to your years. After all, what's a retirement filled with plans and passions if you don't have the health and vigor to enjoy them?

"I Will Survive": The Role of Physical Exercise

In the symphony of your life, your health is the baseline that keeps everything in tune. It's foundational, essential, and frankly, makes everything else sound better. Keeping this baseline groovy requires effort and consciousness about our physical and mental well-being. Yes, it is about preventing and managing ailments but it's also about enhancing your quality of life. Let's face it, you could have all the money and material stuff in the world but if you don't have some modicum of health, how can you enjoy it?

Physical exercise can sometimes feel like a choreographed dance you don't know the steps to. Remember, the goal here isn't to run marathons or bench press twice your body weight (unless that's your jam, of course). It's integrating movement into your life in ways that makes you smile and boost your energy levels. This could be anything from gardening, to yoga, or simple mindful stretches.

The beauty of physical activity is its direct link to improved mood and decreased feelings of depression — not to mention it's a natural energy booster. Think of it as nature's espresso shot. Engaging in regular physical activity helps maintain your independence as you age, and let's be honest, there's a profound joy in being able to lift your own grocery bags or chase after a runaway grand kid at the park or pick up your reading glasses from the floor.

Integrating physical and mental exercises into your daily routine is about finding the right rhythm and pace that suits your lifestyle and preferences. Like a well-composed symphony, a balanced approach to physical and mental well-being can elevate your quality of life, allowing you to engage more fully with the world around you. To help you start on this harmonious path, let's explore some fun and engaging ideas that combines physical and mental stimulation.

"Born to Run": Stay Active with Fun Exercise Routines

Dancing, especially when no one's watching, is one of the most fun ways to stay active. It doesn't require fancy equipment or expensive memberships, just a bit of space, some great music, and a willingness to let go and groove. Start by creating a playlist of your favorite upbeat songs — the ones that make it impossible to sit still.

The beauty of dancing is its dual benefit; not only is it a fantastic physical exercise, helping to improve your balance, strengthen your muscles, and boost cardiovascular health, but it's also a brilliant mood enhancer. The rhythmic movements to the tunes you love can elevate your spirit, reduce stress, and even whisk away feelings of loneliness or melancholy.

Now, while dancing is a blast there are countless other enjoyable ways to stay active. How about turning your daily walk into an exploration? Instead of the same old route, try varying your path or turn your walk into a scavenger hunt by seeking out new landmarks or hidden gems in your neighborhood. Alternatively, consider activities like swimming, which is incredibly gentle on the joints and wonderfully effective in keeping you fit. Or take up cycling, not the Tour de France kind, but leisurely biking around your community or local park. These activities are not just about moving your body; they are adventures and opportunities to discover and engage with the world around you while keeping you physically active.

Setting realistic fitness goals is crucial in maintaining your enthusiasm without feeling overwhelmed. Start by assessing your fitness level and consider what you enjoy most. Your goals should be precise, flexible, measurable, and attainable. This could be something as simple as "I will dance for at least 10 minutes every day" or "I will swim three times a week." Keep track of your progress and celebrate your achievements on a daily basis. Remember, this isn't a competition; it's about building a healthier lifestyle that brings you joy and vitality.

In the spirit of finding that drive and resilience to stay active, let's draw some inspiration from Bruce Springsteen, affectionately known as "The Boss." At an age when many might consider slowing down, he continues to electrify audiences with concerts that exude an energy and passion that many half his age likely envy. His commitment to his fitness and craft provides a powerful lesson in maintaining physical health and vitality. Let "The Boss" inspire you to embrace your physical activities as a celebration of what your body can do, regardless of age.

Reflective Prompt: Think about your favorite ways to move your body. Do you enjoy dancing, walking, swimming, or something else? How could you incorporate these activities into your daily or weekly routine? Write down a plan for integrating more physical activity into your life in a way that feels enjoyable and sustainable.

"Comfortably Numb": Management Retirement Health Concerns

Navigating the waters of health in retirement can feel like the doggy paddle when you really want to be doing a breast stroke. Let's chat about those health concerns that tend to pop up more frequently. It's not the most rock 'n' roll topic, but staying on top of these things can mean more encores in your future!

> Take care of your body. It's the only place you have to live.
>
> Jim Rohn

First, it's a familiar scene for things like arthritis, diabetes, heart conditions, and bone density issues to enter "stage right" during retirement. None of us can turn back the clock (though I wouldn't mind being 25 again with the wisdom of my 60s!), we can manage these conditions with thoughtful lifestyle choices and staying in tune with our bodies. It starts with regular check-ups — think of them as tune-ups for your body, similar to how you'd care for a cherished vintage car. Regular visits to your doctor can help catch any issues while they're still in the opening act, rather than waiting until they're a headline crisis.

Now, let's riff on Pink Floyd's classic "Comfortably Numb." It's a haunting tune that speaks to feeling detached from one's surroundings and self. In our context, it is a powerful metaphor for the danger of disengaging from our health and well-being. The song's narrative could be seen as a wake-up call — a reminder not to let ourselves slip into a state where we ignore what our bodies are trying to tell us. Being 'comfortably numb' might mean ignoring symptoms but just as the song builds to its stirring guitar solo, we can find our crescendo by taking proactive steps to engage fully with our health.

Knowledge about common health issues and the latest medical advancements empowers you to make informed decisions. It's about turning up the volume on health education — whether understanding the side effects of new medications, the benefits of a plant-based diet or research on managing chronic pain. The internet, your doctor, and even health workshops online or at your local community center can be great resources. Think of each piece of information as a note in the broader melody of your health maintenance strategy that supports long-term health and vitality.

So, as Pink Floyd might suggest, let's avoid becoming comfortably numb to our health needs. Instead, let's tune into our bodies, listen to its needs, and rock our days with vigor and vitality. After all, retirement should be about living life to its fullest with intention and care.

Reflective Prompt: Consider any current or potential health challenges you might face as you age. What steps can you take now to manage or prevent these issues? Make a list of actionable steps, such as scheduling regular check-ups, adopting a healthier diet, or starting a new fitness routine.

"I Want to Break Free": Overcome Mind Set Barriers

Retirement, often visualized as an endless summer vacation, can bring its own set of emotional thunderstorms. It's a profound shift, not just in how you spend your days but in how you perceive your role and value in society. Navigating this new terrain might evoke feelings ranging from liberating joy to unsettling anxiety and sometimes, both feelings at once.

For many, a significant hurdle is the loss of identity. You're no longer the manager, the teacher, the nurse or any role that previously defined you and it can feel like you're losing a piece of yourself. Acknowledging that your emotional ups and downs are natural is vital. Like any significant life change, retirement rewrites your routine and expectations, which of course can stir up emotions.

Another common barrier is the fear of irrelevance, the unsettling thought that stepping back from a career equates to stepping back from usefulness. Here, the key is to frame retirement not as a loss but as an opportunity for discovery and reinvention. It's about peeling off those labels to reveal more fundamental aspects of your identity — who you are beyond your previous job title. Building emotional resilience during these times is like strength training your muscles — the more you work on it, the more emotionally robust you become. An effective strategy is to embrace the idea that you are evolving your purpose.

In its soul-stirring capacity, music emerges as a profound ally in managing mental health. It's more than a backdrop for your life; it's a therapeutic tool that can coax out deep-seated emotions and help you put a finger on what you are feeling. What songs have touched you deeply over the years? Chances are these songs reach places words cannot. Creating a "healing playlist" can be a powerful exercise helping you to reflect and express what you are feeling.

Just as a song can move you from tears to laughter, understanding and addressing your mental health can transform your retirement into a more joyful and fulfilling experience. Let music be your companion on this journey, a reminder that every phase of life, like every song, has its highs and lows but ultimately contributes to your life's beautiful melody. Keep tuning into your emotional needs, singing your heart's feelings, and watching your retirement unfold into a masterpiece of well-lived moments.

"Changes": Keep Your Mind Sharp

Now, let's tune into mental exercise — think of it as your brain's daily workout. Just like your body, your mind must stay active to stay sharp. This isn't about doing crosswords until your pen runs out of ink or becoming a chess grand master, though those are great options. It's challenging your brain in ways that are enjoyable and stimulating. It's not rocket science and can be as simple as learning a new recipe, which involves not just the act of cooking but also the art of remembering the steps and measuring the ingredients.

Maintaining a sharp mind is about enriching your day-to-day experience and embracing an insatiable curiosity about the world. The saying "use it or lose it" is absolute truth! Engaging your brain regularly isn't much different from keeping up with your favorite Netflix series or following a beloved book series; it's thrilling, challenges your perceptions, and is deeply satisfying. Let's explore fun and engaging ways to keep your cognitive cogs well-oiled and your mental spark sparking!

Consider digital games like Lumosity or Peak that offer a fun buffet of activities that are designed to train specific cognitive skills. Daily mental challenges can enhance problem-solving skills, improve memory, and speed up processing skills. The key here is the variety — you wouldn't eat the same dinner every night — regularly mixing up your mental workouts can provide the comprehensive brain training that keeps all aspects of your cognition in tip-top shape.

Let's talk about curiosity — your mental fitness's best friend. The beauty of curiosity is that it's an innate part of being human; it doesn't fade with age unless you let it. Staying curious keeps your mind engaged and young, constantly ready to learn and explore. Why not start a curiosity journal? Every day, jot down questions that come to your mind about anything and everything. Why is the sky blue? What is a black hole? What's the story behind my favorite song? Then, take the time to research and discover the answers. This practice keeps your research skills sharp and continuously expands your knowledge base.

Documentaries and podcasts are another fantastic way to feed your curiosity. Another unique option are sleuthing websites like Websleuths™. Everybody loves a good mystery and some internet users have taken that to the next level. Sleuthing forums and online crime-solving groups have emerged across the web letting ordinary people help solve high-profile and cold cases.

These platforms can satiate any intellectual appetite with topics ranging from history and science to art and true crime. They're like a mental gymnasium, where each new piece of information adds weight to your cognitive barbell. And the best part? You can dive into these learning adventures from the comfort of your couch, during a long walk, or while pottering around in the garden.

As you continue to write the following chapters of your life, remember that keeping your mind sharp is more than retaining memory or improving focus — it's about enhancing the quality of every moment. So be curious of the world around you and let your mind flex its muscles to the rhythm of lifelong learning and discovery.

Take Away

As we've danced through this chapter together, tuning into the rhythms of physical and mental wellness, we've explored how embracing a healthy lifestyle in retirement can be much like crafting a beautiful melody. The key takeaway? Your health is not just a series of statistics or medical reports; it's the essence of your daily experiences influencing every moment and memory.

Activity: The Playlist Workout Challenge

Ready to shake things up? Here's a playful challenge that will add a bit of zest to your routine. I call it the "Playlist Workout Challenge" and the best part, it kills two birds at once. You create jamming playlists as a backdrop to your physical exercise and the process itself is an exercise for that muscle between your ears. It's simple, fun and you can do it right in your living room. Here's how it works:

Create a Playlist: Put together a playlist of three to five of your favorite upbeat songs. These should be tunes that make you want to move. Think "Dancing Queen" by ABBA or "Eye of the Tiger" by Survivor — songs with a good beat.

Set Your Timer: Each song will be a different workout segment. The idea is to move continuously from one song to the next, doing simple exercises that match the beat. Start with gentle movement and get progressively more strenuous.

Get Creative: Use the rhythm of the music to guide your movements. You can sway, move your arms, dance, jog on the spot or even throw in some air guitar for fun. The key is to keep moving and enjoy the music.

Cool Down: Use the final song to slow things down and bring your mini workout to a graceful close.

This exercise is not only a great way to get some physical activity, but it also stimulates your brain. Remembering the sequence of exercises, keeping up with the rhythm, and enjoying your favorite tunes are all fantastic ways to keep your body and mind in top form. So, lace up your sneakers, crank up the tunes, and let's get moving. Your retirement is the "Monterey Pop Festival" of your life and you want to be in the best shape — physically and mentally — to enjoy every last bit of it. Let the music lead the way!

Coming to the close of this chapter, remember, each small, positive step to improve your physical and mental fitness is reflected in the quality of each and every day in your life. Let the dance of health continue with you, my dear reader, leading the way.

Side note: I initially had "your retirement is the *Woodstock* festival" of your life but my editor mentioned not everybody enjoyed Woodstock. Really? So I switched to the Monterey Pop Festival, in my hometown of Monterey, California and discovered a few interesting facts I didn't know until I wrote this section!

Monterey Pop Festival (1967)

Location: Monterey, California
Highlights: This was a defining moment for the "Summer of Love" and introduced the U.S. to legendary artists like Jimi Hendrix, Janis Joplin, and The Who.
Significance: Known as one of the first major rock festivals, it set the stage for Woodstock and other festivals that followed.

CHAPTER FOUR

BUILD AND NURTURE SOCIAL CONNECTIONS

I magine retirement as a block party and your social connections are the guests. Some are lively dancers, spinning through your days with laughter and stories; others are like the comfort of a well-worn sofa, always there to offer support and a listening ear. This chapter is about ensuring your party is splendid and fulfilling, filled with meaningful interactions and supportive relationships. After all, what's a celebration without the company of good friends and family?

The people in your life can turn a simple melody into a rich symphony. Social connections in retirement aren't just the icing on the cake; they are main ingredients that make life sweet, vibrant, and wonderfully complex. This chapter explores how you can build and nurture these relationships to enhance your well-being, find joy in shared experiences, and create a support network of mutual respect, understanding, and love.

"You're My Best Friend": Reconnecting with Old Friends Post-Retirement

Let's start with the friends who have been the baseline of your life's soundtrack — those who've been with you through thick and thin. Connecting with old friends can be like rediscovering a classic album; it's familiar, brings back memories, and feels like coming home. But as we all know, time can change the tempo of even the strongest friendships. People evolve, circumstances shift, and what was once a daily coffee chat might now be a yearly catch-up call.

Revitalizing these relationships often means reaching out, even stepping out of your comfort zone. Send that text, make that call, or write a brief note and send via mail. Invite them over Zoom for a cup of tea or a glass of wine. Share your new adventures, ask about theirs, and gently rekindle the connection that once was. Not every attempt will lead to a renewed friendship, but the joy of those that do bloom again is often worth the effort.

The key is approaching this process with patience and an open heart. When reaching out to old friends, start with a simple message or call that doesn't demand much in return. It could be a fond memory you shared or an article you think they'd enjoy. Remember, not every outreach will lead to a rekindled friendship. Still, occasionally, you'll strike a chord that revives a beautiful melody you both enjoyed. These moments often remind us why these friendships mattered in the first place.

As we rekindle these old friendships, it's important to acknowledge and accept the changes that time has brought. We're not the same people we were 10, 20, or 30 years ago, and that's okay. Embrace the new stories and experiences your friends bring to the table. Celebrate the growth, the wisdom, and the journeys you've both undertaken. This mutual respect for each other's paths can strengthen the bond you share, creating a deeper, more meaningful connection.

Don't be afraid to inject a little fun and spontaneity into the process. Plan a virtual movie night with your favorite films from back in the day, or start a book club with the novels you've always meant to read. Reminisce about the good old days, but also look forward to creating new memories together. This blend of nostalgia and fresh experiences can rejuvenate your friendship and make it even more rewarding.

As you navigate this journey of reconnecting, remember that it's not about quantity but quality. Even if you rekindle just one or two old friendships, the joy and comfort these relationships bring can enrich your retirement immensely. These friends, who have seen you through various stages of life, can offer a unique perspective and understanding that newer acquaintances might not.

In the end, reconnecting with old friends is about honoring the shared history while embracing the present and future. It's about creating a harmonious blend of past and present, much like a beautifully remixed song. So, take that step, reach out, and rediscover the cherished connections that have been the baseline of your life's soundtrack. Reviving these friendships will add a vibrant, fulfilling dimension to your retirement journey.

Reflective Prompt: Make a list of friends or acquaintances you've lost touch with but would like to reconnect with. Think about why these relationships were important to you. What small step could you take this week to reach out to one of these individuals?

"Girls Just Wanna Have Fun": Making New Friends Post-Retirement

Now, imagine adding new songs to your favorite playlist. Just as a fresh tune can bring a new vibe, new friends can bring fresh perspectives and energy into your life. Meeting new people might seem daunting, but it's also exhilarating. Think of it as an adventure — an opportunity to learn, grow, and expand your social circle. But where do you start?

First, consider your interests and passions. Are you a bookworm, a gardening enthusiast, or a budding artist? Joining clubs, classes, or online forums related to your hobbies is a fantastic way to meet like-minded people. You'll find that shared interests provide a natural starting point for conversations and connections. Plus, you get the added bonus of indulging in activities you love while making new friends.

Don't underestimate the power of volunteering. Giving your time to causes you care about not only feels great but also puts you in touch with others who share your values and dedication. Whether it's at a local animal shelter, a community garden, or a hospital, volunteering opens doors to meaningful relationships and enriches your life in unexpected ways. And let's be honest, there's nothing like bonding over a shared mission to save the puppies or plant more trees!

Another fun way to meet new people is through travel. Joining a travel group or taking organized day trips can lead to friendships with fellow adventurers. Exploring new places together creates lasting memories and fosters a sense of camaraderie. You never know, you might just find your new best friend while hiking up a scenic trail or marveling at a historical landmark.

Technology, despite its occasional frustrations, can be a great ally in making new friends. Social media platforms, online communities, and even apps designed for meeting new people can connect you with individuals from all over the world. It's like having a global social club at your fingertips. So, don't be shy — send that friend request, join that online book club, or participate in that virtual cooking class.

As you embark on this journey of making new friends, remember to be open and authentic. Show genuine interest in others, share your stories, and be willing to step out of your comfort zone. It's not about collecting a large number of friends but forming meaningful connections. Each new friendship adds a unique note to the melody of your life, enhancing its richness and diversity.

In the end, making new friends post-retirement is about embracing the unknown and welcoming new experiences with open arms. So, get out there, be bold, and let the adventure of meeting new friends begin. Your social symphony will be all the more beautiful for it.

"With a Little Help from My Friends": The Magic of Shared Activities

Shared activities are the cornerstone of building and nurturing relationships. They provide common ground and a chance to create the baseline for deeper connections. Whether it's a weekly golf outing or a music appreciation class, these activities allow you to bond over shared passions and interests. Moreover, these gatherings are often accompanied by laughter, stories, and mutual support, enriching your social life and providing a sense of community and belonging. They remind us that we're not just individuals living in isolation but part of a vibrant collective of lives, each unique yet beautifully interconnected.

Finding your tribe in retirement may not feel comfortable for you to do but it's relatively easy — connect your interests and passions with those of others. Start by listing what excites you — hiking, gardening, music, painting, pottery — and seek out local clubs or online communities that share these interests. Websites like Meetup can be a treasure trove for finding groups that get together for everything from hiking to book discussions. When you attend these gatherings, bring your whole self to the table. Share your stories, ask genuine questions, and listen actively. This kind of engagement often leads to invitations to other events or introductions to like-minded folks.

The joy in shared activities can't be overstated. Doing what you love alongside others enhances your skills and builds a community of peers who share your enthusiasm. These activities provide natural topics for conversation and bonding, reducing the pressure that sometimes accompanies new social interactions. They also have a way of multiplying joy — the laughter is louder, the insights are more profound, and the experiences are richer when shared.

Finally, remember that the power of shared activities lies in the connections you form and the memories you create. These experiences foster a sense of belonging and continuity, helping you maintain a positive outlook and a resilient spirit throughout your retirement. Embrace these opportunities to engage with others, and you'll find that your retirement years are rich with meaningful relationships and joyful experiences.

"Unwritten": Building Your Relationships

Think of your social life as a symphony, where each relationship plays a distinct part in creating a harmonious whole. Some friends are the brass section — loud and energizing. Other friends may be more like the string section offering a warm embrace of support and comfort. And then the rare instruments, unique and a bit quirky but absolutely essential to the richness of the ensemble.

Building and nurturing this symphony means conducting these relationships with care and intention. It involves listening attentively, participating earnestly, and appreciating each person's contribution to your life. This means making time for your relationships, through regular get togethers, phone calls, or simply sending a thoughtful message to ensure that your connections remain strong and vibrant.

But it's equally important to recognize when a relationship is not beneficial to your well-being and growth. Just as a sour note can disrupt a beautiful melody, a toxic relationship can impact your overall happiness and peace. It's okay to step back or even end connections that drain your energy, cause stress, or hinder your personal growth. Your well-being should always come first.

Learning to figure out which relationships to nurture and which to let go is a big part of building a fulfilling social life. Creating a balanced and supportive environment for yourself means you have to set boundaries and that may mean you decide to distance yourself from the people and things that upset the balance of harmony in your life.

In the end, your social symphony is a reflection of the love, respect, and joy you share with others. Embrace the journey, cherish each note, and let the music of your social life play on.

"You Can't Always Get What You Want": Navigate Social Expectations

Diving into the social scene of retirement can be like turning up at a buffet laden with more dishes than you could sample. You might find yourself yearning to taste everything! Yet reality will absolutely remind us that our appetites — in this case, for social connections and activities — might exceed what's on our plate. Managing expectations becomes crucial in avoiding a sort of social indigestion, where you end up feeling overwhelmed or underwhelmed by the friendships and community involvement at your disposal.

Let's face it, only some social gatherings will be a hit, not every new acquaintance will become a bosom buddy, and some long-anticipated community events might fall flat. That's perfectly alright. Part of navigating this new social landscape is learning to adjust your expectations, understanding that while you can steer your social life in a particular direction, you can't control every outcome. Finding fulfillment in what is available and attainable is perhaps the sweetest and most challenging skill to master in retirement. It's about cherishing the depth of a few close friends over a wide, but shallow network. It's really about being the authority of your social life — selecting what truly enriches you and letting go of what does not. This might mean saying no to a social obligation that feels more draining than fulfilling, or it might involve stepping back from a volunteer role that no longer aligns with your interests or values.

Contentment comes from cultivating gratitude for the relationships and opportunities that add value to your life. It's the laughter shared over a game of cards, the solace in a heartfelt conversation, or the sense of achievement from a completed community project. In navigating the social expectations of retirement, embrace the journey with an open heart and a flexible mindset. You'll discover that the social connections you cultivate can become one of the most rewarding aspects of your retirement life.

Reflective Prompt: Think about your social life now verses what you envision it could be. Are there specific social expectations you feel pressured to meet that don't align with your desires? How might you redefine your social interactions to better match your personal values and interests?

"Lean on Me": The Importance of Support Networks

Building a support network means combining a variety of relationships — each distinct but crucial. Start with family members who often form the foundation of a support network. Open lines of communication about your needs and aspirations and how they can be part of your vibrant retirement life. It's more than asking for help; it's about sharing your journey and making them a part of your ongoing story. Extend this network by reconnecting with old friends and nurturing new ones. These people add unique rhythms and harmonies, offering different perspectives and experiences that enrich your life.

Community members form another essential part of your support network. These might be neighbors, fellow volunteers, or members of local clubs you belong to. Building these connections involves more than casual chats over the fence. It's about engaging, showing up, and offering your skills or time. When you invest in your community, the community invests in you, providing support in ways you might not have anticipated — from helping you with household tasks to offering companionship and moral support during challenging times.

Moreover, pay attention to the potential of digital communities. Online forums, social media groups, and virtual clubs can also be part of your support network, especially if mobility or distance makes it challenging to engage in person. These platforms allow you to stay connected, share experiences, and receive support from like-minded individuals across the globe. Whether it's a retirement group on Facebook or a virtual book club, these digital spaces can offer companionship and advice at the click of a button.

Asking for help, while sometimes daunting, is a critical aspect of nurturing and utilizing your support network. It requires acknowledging that independence doesn't mean going it alone. Reaching out is a sign of strength, whether needing a ride to an appointment, help with a home improvement project, or simply someone to talk to after a rough day. It shows a healthy self-awareness and trust in the bonds you've cultivated. People want to help but need to know what you need. Being open about your needs allows your network to function effectively, providing timely and tailored support to your situation.

The strength of a support network lies in its collective power. The beauty of this collective strength is that it's reciprocal. You contribute to your network as much as you rely on it. Whether offering wise counsel or lending a listening ear, your involvement adds to the network's resilience and capacity to support others. In this way, the support system becomes a dynamic, living entity, evolving and strengthening with each exchange and interaction.

Reflective Prompt: Evaluate your current support network. Who are the key people you can lean on for emotional, practical, and social support? Are there gaps you would like to fill? What steps could you take to strengthen your support network?

"Bridge Over Troubled Water": Being There for Others in Tough Times

Navigating the currents of life, especially during its more turbulent moments, requires a delicate balance of giving and receiving support. Imagine you're on a long hike with a group of friends, and suddenly, one of them stumbles. You wouldn't hesitate to extend a hand, offer a comforting word, or even share your water. This instinctive response to support those in need is profoundly human and deeply necessary. It affirms our connections and reinforces our communal bonds through acts of kindness and understanding.

Empathy lies at the heart of all supportive relationships. It's the ability to put yourself in someone else's shoes, to feel with them, and to see the world from their perspective. This emotional connection is so important in building stronger and deeper bonds between people. I would venture to say that we need so much more of this in the world. A simple act of kindness, to a friend or a complete stranger can touch them in ways we may never know. And just as true, a hateful comment can profoundly wound.

Each gesture of support, no matter its size, has the potential to significantly impact someone's life. Consider, for instance, the simple act of preparing a meal for a grieving friend. This act goes beyond nourishing their body — it's a statement that "you are not alone" in the struggle and that their well-being matters to you. Sometimes, the most powerful support you can offer is your presence. Just being there for someone can speak volumes in a way that words sometimes cannot.

In these acts of support, empathy, and presence, you comfort others and reinforce the strength of your social connections. Being there for someone else highlights the reciprocal nature of support networks, reminding us that we are all part of a larger community. Whether through a comforting embrace, a listening ear, or a shoulder to lean on, these connections underscore the profound impact we have on each other's lives, proving that sometimes, the simplest forms of support are the most enduring.

Take Away

To help you visualize and organize your social connections, let's create your "Social Playlist." This fun exercise allows you to see the variety and richness of your social life at a glance. It helps you identify areas where you might want to add a new tune or fine-tune the harmony.

Activity: Social Playlist

List Your Social Activities: Start by listing all your regular social activities. Next to each activity, note the people you interact with and how you feel about these interactions. Are they uplifting, draining, or neutral?

Categorize Your Relationships: Next, categorize these relationships into different sections of your playlist. For example, you might have sections like "Family Ties," "Old Friends," "New Acquaintances," and "Community Connections."

Identify Gaps: Look at your categories and see if there are any gaps. Do you need connections in certain areas of interest? Are there activities you wish to explore that are outside your social repertoire?

Set Goals for Social Growth: Set one or two goals for developing your social connections. For example, you can make one new friend in the next month or join a new club or group that aligns with your interests.

Review Regularly: Every few months, revisit your Social Playlist. Add new friends, update your feelings about specific activities and adjust your goals. This keeps your social life dynamic and responsive to your evolving interests and needs.

This exercise encourages you to be proactive in nurturing and expanding your social circle. Just like a DJ tweaks their playlist to suit the mood or the event, you can adjust your Social Playlist to enhance the quality and satisfaction of your social life. After all, life is better when shared, and your retirement should be no exception.

As we close this chapter, remember that the symphony of your retirement is most beautiful when played in concert with friends and loved ones. Each relationship contributes a unique note to the melody of your days, creating a richer, more harmonious life experience. So, reach out, connect, and share this incredible journey with those around you.

Looking ahead, our next chapter will explore the enriching world of lifelong learning in retirement, proving you absolutely CAN teach an old dog new tricks!

CHAPTER FIVE

CULTIVATE LIFELONG LEARNING

Welcome to my favorite place in the world — lifelong learning, where curiosity never fades and every day offers a new opportunity to expand your knowledge. The path to being a lifelong learner is not a solitary pursuit; it can be a journey that connects you with diverse experiences and people, enriching your life with every new encounter.

As you go through this chapter, think of yourself as an explorer exploring new territories that may not be in the world around you but within the realms of knowledge and experience. Whether it's exploring the mysteries of the universe, mastering a new skill, or simply learning how to cook a new cuisine, every learning opportunity is a step towards a more fulfilling and engaged life.

So, dust off your library card, tune up your curiosity and prepare to see retirement through the lens of continuous discovery and joy. After all, the mind is not a vessel to be filled but a fire to be kindled. Let's stoke the fire with the kindling of knowledge and watch as it illuminates your world in dazzling ways.

"Forever Young": Cultivating a Mindset for New Adventures

Embracing lifelong learning involves more than just signing up for a class or reading a book; it requires building a mindset open to new ideas, challenges, and changes. Think of your mindset as fertile soil. You wouldn't go flinging seeds around and expect a bountiful harvest — you prepare with intention. Before planting, you cultivate the soil, making sure it's rich and ready for planting. In the same way, nurturing a mindset for learning requires a sense of wonder and curiosity, along with a willingness to embrace the unexpected. By doing this, you ensure that what you plant can truly take root and flourish.

One effective approach to learning is to come at it as if you know nothing, even in areas you are familiar with. This approach is the essence of a "beginner's mind". By embracing this mindset, you stay open to new insights and free yourself from the mental rigidity that often shapes our working lives. Be willing to admit that you don't know everything and feel excited and curious to fill those gaps — whatever they may be. A fun and powerful way to discover what you might want to explore is by asking yourself this: "If *[fill in the blank]* had or hadn't happened, what would I have liked to do, be, or experience?" Taking the time to reflect on these "what ifs" can uncover hidden passions or interests you may never have given yourself the chance to explore before. This openness to possibility is where true growth happens, and it's where the joy of learning truly begins.

Another crucial aspect of preparing your mindset for learning is resilience. Along the way, you'll have successes, but also unexpected detours that lead to learning something entirely different than what you intended. You might find quantum physics dull or struggle with the tricky pronunciations in Italian, and that's perfectly fine. Sometimes, exploring a topic leads to amazing discoveries; other times, you just chase a "squirrel". Being resilient and flexible means not letting those "squirrel" moments define your learning journey, but actually allowing them to enhance it.

Happily, lifelong learning is not a solo expedition. It thrives on the exchange of ideas and experiences. Engaging with others through study groups, online forums, or community classes can profoundly enhance learning experiences. These social interactions make learning more enjoyable and deepen your understanding by exposing you to different perspectives and insights. They transform learning from a solitary activity into a community activity.

Reflective Prompt: What subjects, skills, or hobbies have you always been curious about but never had the chance to pursue? List three new things you'd like to learn about or try in the next year. What steps can you take today to start exploring one of these interests?

"She Blinded Me with Science": Embracing Technology as a Learning Tool

Technology plays a pivotal role in lifelong learning in today's digital age. It offers unprecedented access to information and learning resources that previous generations could only dream of. From online courses on platforms like Udemy, Coursera and Khan Academy to educational videos on YouTube, to apps for just about everything, all on a hand-held device like a phone, tablet or iPad. The ease of access to high level learning via technology has never been more flexible and diverse. Of course, it's important to note that you must be diligent and alert to the risks of technology. For instance, you get an email with invoice details for a PayPal purchase you know you didn't make, offering a phone number to call should you wish to dispute it. Your gut tells you something isn't right so instead of calling the phone number in the email you check your PayPal account directly and find there is no charge and confirm this is absolutely a scam. So eyes wide open!

For many, technology can feel like a double-edged sword — both enticing and intimidating. The key is to approach technology with curiosity rather than fear. Start by figuring out what you want to do, that will show you what tools or devices you'll need. For example, if you're interested in painting, you might want to take a class on your computer versus your phone. Begin by deciding what you want to do (learn) and then you'll be better able to decide what device will work best. Once you figure that out, learning the basics, whether it's navigating a computer, smartphone, tablet, or iPad, will build your skills and let technology be a valuable ally in your learning journey.

Remember lifelong learning isn't just accumulating knowledge. It's about enriching your life, connecting with others, and embracing the endless joy of discovering something new.

Keep your mind active, your heart open, and your curiosity alive and you'll find that learning is not just a part of life — it's one of the best parts!

"Electric Avenue": Learn Through Online Courses and Local Classes

Imagine strolling through a marketplace of ideas, instructors, and teachers all ready to share their knowledge and insights. This marketplace isn't a figment of imagination — it's the thriving world of information, online programs, courses and listings for local classes, that are designed to keep your mind as agile as a ninja. Life long learning is a gym membership for your brain; it enriches you mentally, brings personal satisfaction, and enhances your social life by connecting you with fellow knowledge seekers.

Online learning platforms might seem as daunting as decoding an alien transmission but they're really more like friendly librarians eager to guide you through the virtual aisles of topics and subjects. Learning platforms, like Udemy and MasterClass, offer courses on everything from astrophysics to perfecting your zucchini bread recipe. Whatever piques your interest, there's something for everyone, no matter how niche or mainstream your curiosity might be.

Online platforms are particularly appealing because they allow you to learn at your own pace, from the comfort of your home. You can dive into the intricacies of ancient history or the basics of backyard barbecues while in your pajamas with a cup of coffee by your side. Class Central and Coursera are learning hubs offer free online classes for seniors where courses are your open window to new ideas and you hold an open ticket.

But let's remember the vibrant learning opportunities outside your doorstep! Local classes and workshops at community colleges, libraries, and community centers often include access to resources that might not be available at home, like specialized tools, professional guidance from instructors, and the collective wisdom of fellow classmates.

Each class becomes a mini-adventure, a shared journey into learning with others who are excited to explore new territories of knowledge. Whether learning how to throw pottery, mastering a new language, or understanding the nuances of wine tasting, each class offers a unique blend of education and social interaction, making learning a fun, rewarding communal activity.

Many community centers and libraries are attuned to the interests and needs of retirees, offering courses during convenient times and fostering an environment of inclusivity and respect for all ages. They often provide courses beyond mere hobbies, offering practical skills to enhance your daily life, such as nutrition classes tailored to senior health or technology workshops that demystify the digital world.

The beauty of engaging with online platforms and local classes lies in their blend of convenience and community. While online courses allow you to learn at your own pace and choose from an almost limitless array of topics, local classes offer the invaluable experience of face-to-face interaction and the spontaneous joy of shared learning experiences. Together, they create a comprehensive educational environment that keeps your mind sharp, your heart engaged, and your social life bustling.

Whether you explore the ancient mysteries of Egypt from your laptop or get your hands dirty in a pottery class with new friends, the world of lifelong learning is rich with opportunities to keep you young at heart. Embrace these chances to expand your horizons, and you'll find that every day brings a new reason to love this unencumbered stage of life.

"It's Only Rock and Roll (But I Like It)": Tech Savvy Retirees

Wielding technology is like learning anything new. It may feel awkward at first and you will have challenges, but once you have the basic skills a world of possibilities opens up. My "device of choice" is a desktop PC with two 32-inch displays. For me, doing anything more on my smartphone beyond calls or texts is a recipe for frustration (it doesn't help they call them smartphones). My point is, get comfortable with the device you choose for what you want to do and with some practice you'll be using your "device of choice" confidently.

Once you have the basics, it's time to explore the vast online resources. Websites like YouTube, TechBoomers and GCFGlobal, and countless more, offer free tutorials covering everything from art to zoology! These resources allow you to learn independently, revisit lessons as needed, and gradually build a comfortable proficiency with everyday digital tools. It's like having a private tutor ready at your beckon call!

Let's talk about applying these newfound skills to enhance your life. Imagine connecting with your family, friends and grandchildren via video calls. Imagine discovering a new passion with digital photography and creating digital scrapbooks. Imagine managing your medical records and appointments with a few clicks. Each activity enriches your life and brings a sense of accomplishment and independence. Moreover, for those with entrepreneurial spirits, the digital world offers platforms to start online businesses or blogs, turning hobbies into potential income streams, or simply a way to share your passions with the world.

However, with great connectivity comes great responsibility, especially regarding online safety and privacy. Navigating the internet safely is crucial. Let's face it: scams have been around before the invention of the wheel and in the online world they can be taken to new heights. Just like the real world, common sense is your biggest ally in staying safe on the internet. You wouldn't stand at an ATM and enter your bank pin number with a stranger looking over your shoulder right? Protecting yourself starts with understanding the basics of online security — simple practices like creating strong, unique passwords for each account, and being wary of unsolicited emails asking for personal information is just the start. Consider investing time in an online security course or attending a workshop at your local community center. These can provide valuable tips and habits for safe browsing and online interactions, ensuring you can enjoy the benefits of the digital world with lower risks.

In embracing the digital age, you're not just keeping up with the times; you're opening doors to a world of connectivity, creativity, and independence. From the practicalities of managing everyday tasks to the joys of exploring new hobbies and staying in touch with loved ones, becoming tech-savvy is your backstage pass to a world of possibilities.

Reflective Prompt: What is your comfort level with technology? What digital skills do you want to get better at? What resources (such as classes, online tutorials, or help from a friend) could you use to begin? Write down a simple tech goal for the next month.

"Learning to Fly": Virtual Reality — Experience History, Art, and Science

Stepping into Virtual Reality (VR) feels like slipping through a secret door into alternate universes where the impossible becomes your playground. Imagine being able to soar through the skies, stroll through ancient cities, or dive deep into the ocean — all without leaving your living room! It's not just technology — it's exhilarating experiences waiting to be had. Forget sitting on the sidelines; VR immerses you, reigniting your sense of wonder and curiosity in a way you never thought possible.

While it may be a little intimidating to begin there are several options on the market, each with its features and price points. Opting for user-friendly models like the Oculus Quest or the HTC Vive Cosmos is a great start. These devices are known for their straightforward setup and ease of use. Depending on the headset model, you may also need a compatible device, usually a smartphone or computer. I've included additional information in the Appendix at the end of the book.

Once your setup is complete, the real adventures start. VR technology is revolutionizing learning by making it a fully immersive, interactive experience. Imagine stepping into a virtual art class where you can view Van Gogh's Starry Night and watch the artist as he paints, discussing his techniques and inspirations. This active participation deepens your understanding and retention of information. It's about being in the moment, whether walking alongside dinosaurs in a prehistoric landscape or standing in the Sistine Chapel, looking up at Michelangelo's ceiling frescoes.

Virtual Reality also offers incredible explorations in science and nature. For anyone who has ever dreamed of exploring the cosmos or diving into the ocean's depths, VR makes these journeys possible from your living room. You can embark on a guided tour of the human body, exploring the intricate workings of the heart or the brain's complex structure. For nature enthusiasts, dive into the Great Barrier Reef and observe marine life in its natural habitat without getting wet.

These scientific explorations are fascinating and make complex concepts accessible and engaging. They allow you to experience art, history and science in ways that books and traditional media cannot offer, providing a hands-on understanding that can ignite a life-long passion for learning about the past, present and future. It also presents a wonderful opportunity to take a grandchild or friend along with you!

As you explore Virtual Reality, you'll find it enhances your knowledge and sparks a sense of wonder and excitement about learning. It's a testament to how technology can improve our understanding of the world in profound and engaging ways. VR offers a new horizon in lifelong learning, where the possibilities are as limitless as your curiosity. So, take the leap, set up your VR gear, and prepare to immerse yourself into landscapes of knowledge you've only ever dreamed of exploring.

Reflective Prompt: Think about any apprehensions you might have regarding technology. What are the top three things that intimidate you the most about using new tech tools? How might you overcome these fears? What support or resources do you need to feel more comfortable?

"Space Oddity": Virtual Travel — Explore the World from Your Living Room

When it comes to travel think of Virtual Reality as your personal teleportation device. It's travel without the constraints, and for retirees who may face mobility or health challenges, it's an incredible way to reclaim the joy and freedom of exploring new destinations.

Imagine sipping your morning coffee in the cozy comfort of your favorite armchair, then putting on a headset and suddenly finding yourself virtually strolling through the cobbled streets of Paris or standing beneath the towering expanse of the Grand Canyon. This isn't the plot of a science fiction novel; it's the reality offered by today's VR technology, bringing the world to your doorstep in vivid, breathtaking detail.

Picture this: one moment, you're in your living room; the next, you're in a virtual museum tour! VR is revolutionizing how we interact with art and culture. Institutions like the British Museum in London and the Smithsonian in Washington, D.C., offer virtual tours that showcase their collections and provide rich multimedia content such as videos, audio guides, and detailed textual descriptions. This approach allows you to dive deep into the stories behind the exhibits, learning about their historical contexts, artistic techniques, and cultural significance engagingly and educationally.

These virtual experiences can be guided and interactive, or free-range allowing you to choose your path and explore at your own pace. Some platforms even offer live-streamed tours where guides lead you through real locations in real time, answering your questions and sharing insights just as they would on a physical tour. This interactive element adds a layer of personalization and connection to the experience, making it more than just a visual journey — it becomes a dynamic exploration where your curiosity leads the way.

In embracing Virtual Reality, you embrace a world where the boundaries of age, mobility, and geography no longer dictate your ability to explore and enjoy the planet's most extraordinary sights and experiences. It's a testament to the power of technology to broaden our horizons and deepen our understanding of the world in which we live. So, go ahead, put on that headset, and let the adventure begin. Who knows where you'll go today? Whether it's the peaks of distant mountains or the depths of the ocean's heart, the world awaits and is as close as your living room.

Take Away

As we wrap up this enlightening chapter on keeping your mind active through learning, let's distill it down to its essence: Lifelong learning is more than accumulating facts and figures; it's about enriching your daily experience, connecting deeply with the world around you, and keeping your cognitive wheels greased and ready to roll. Every lesson learned, every new skill acquired, and every virtual journey taken adds layers to your symphony, making it richer and more beautiful.

To put all these insights into action, I'd like to introduce an enjoyable and practical activity called the "Learning Explorer's Journal." This exercise is designed to help you apply and reflect on the learning strategies we've discussed, making them a tangible and regular part of your life. Here's how you can start:

Activity: Learning Explorer's Journal

Create Your Journal: Choose a notebook or digital app where you can comfortably and regularly record your learning adventures. This journal is your personal space to explore, reflect, and grow.

Set Weekly Learning Goals: At the start of each week, set a realistic learning goal. It could be anything from watching a documentary on a subject you know little about to completing an online course or even visiting a virtual museum.

Daily Insights: Dedicate a few minutes each day to jot down what you've learned. Did you discover something surprising? Did a particular piece of information challenge your previous beliefs? How does this new knowledge connect with your existing experiences?

Reflect: At the end of the week, reflect on how you can apply the knowledge gained. If you've learned a new gardening technique, think about how you might use it in your garden.

Emotional Response: Learning isn't just intellectual; it's also emotional. Record how each learning experience made you feel. Inspired? Confused? Excited? Reflecting on these emotions can deepen your engagement with the material and enhance your learning experience.

Adjust and Adapt: Learning is a dynamic process. At the end of each month, review your journal entries. What topics did you enjoy? Which learning formats worked best for you? Adjust your goals and methods based on these insights to make future learning more effective and enjoyable.

This "Learning Explorer's Journal" encourages you to see every day as an opportunity to learn something new, expand your horizons, and meaningfully engage with the world. It's a tool that tracks what you know and how you grow and change due to your explorations.

As we close this chapter, remember, the world is brimming with knowledge and every piece of information you gather lights up a previously dark corner of your universe. Keep your curiosity alive, your mind open, and your heart ready to embrace the vast wonders of learning. The journey doesn't end; it only gets more fascinating, paving the way to a more enriched, more enlightened you.

The next chapter will focus on creating a harmonious living space that reflects your style and supports your well-being. It takes the insights from the world you've explored through learning and reflects them back into your everyday surroundings. Let's prepare to make your living environment as enriched and engaging as your mind.

CHAPTER SIX

CREATE A HARMONIOUS LIVING SPACE

In this chapter, we're not just arranging furniture or hanging curtains but creating spaces that wrap around you like a warm hug when you walk in. Rooms that spark joy and invite peace. Corners where each item tells a story of your life's adventures. This is about creating a harmonious living space that sings in tune with your soul and resonates with your personal melody.

Creating a personal sanctuary doesn't require the Midas touch or an interior designer's diploma. It's creating a space where your personality, memories, and dreams supports your well-being and reflects your journey. Maybe it's transforming a cluttered study into a serene reading nook or rearranging your living room to create a flow that welcomes you every time you walk into it.

This chapter is about improving how you feel at home by creating spaces that lifts your spirit, comforts your heart, and stimulates your mind. As we explore the art of crafting such a place, remember, your home is the most personal artwork you'll ever create. It's a living expression of your unique taste, experiences, and joys.

"Our House": Personalization, not Perfection

Before diving into the practical aspects of creating your harmonious living space, let's start with some visualization. Find a place where you won't be interrupted, close your eyes and imagine walking through your ideal home. Don't sweat it if you're not getting crystal clear pictures of the space. Notice the colors surrounding you, the textures you may feel under your fingertips, and the artwork on the walls. What aromas would you want to greet you as you enter? Sandalwood? Patchouli? How is the light filtering through the windows? Do you light a candle before you sit down to enjoy this space? This mental walk-through is your blueprint, the dream upon which you'll create your reality.

Keep this vision in mind as we go through the practical steps to bring it to life. From de-cluttering to choosing the right colors, from optimizing your space for comfort and utility to selecting decorations that speak to your soul, each step is a deliberate, joyful act of creation. Your home is more than just a place to live; it's a space to thrive, dream, and find peace. Let's make it a reflection of who you are and what you aspire to be.

Now, before you get overwhelmed thinking you have to tackle the entire house at once, take a deep breath. Start small. Pick one room or even just one corner of a room. Maybe it's that cozy reading nook you've always wanted or the kitchen counter that could use a bit of de-cluttering. By focusing on small, manageable areas, you can gradually extend your personal touch throughout your home without feeling like you're staging an all-out renovation war. Plus, small victories add up and keep the momentum going.

As you begin, remember that the goal is not perfection but personalization. You're not creating a showroom; you're crafting a sanctuary for yourself! This journey is taking a space and making it your own. A haven that shelters your body and nurtures your spirit. Keep your vision in mind, let your heart lead the way, and you'll transform your home into a harmonious masterpiece of spaces that sings to your soul.

In Appendix A I've included *7 Practical Steps to Get Started Creating a Harmonious Living Space* that I hope you'll find useful throughout this chapter.

"Home": Declutter and Organization

De-cluttering plays a pivotal role in creating your sanctuary by reclaiming your space and, by extension, your life. Start by evaluating each item and asking whether it serves a purpose or brings you joy. If the answer is no, let it go. This doesn't mean stripping your home bare! If the answer is "I don't know", make a "idk" pile, add the item and keep on moving. You can circle back around to your "idk" pile later! The focus to keep is this: *"you are choosing to surround yourself with the things that add value to your life, whether functional or emotional."*

Imagine opening your closet and feeling that familiar weight of overwhelm. Most people, when they open their bedroom closet, or any closet for that matter, see a space clogged with clothes and other stuff, usually in semi-darkness because if you do have a closet light, it doesn't penetrate through the clutter. It's a feeling of being suffocated by things that no longer serve you.

Now, picture this instead: you open your closet and see only things you love! Every item sparks joy, and there's a sense of calm and clarity. The clothes are neatly arranged, making it easy to find what you need. The light reaches every corner. It's like a breath of fresh air every time you open the door. No more stress, just a feeling of peace and satisfaction. Welcome to the liberating world of "letting go" — where less really is more. You're not stripping away joys or memories; you're honing in on what truly enhances your life and making space for new experiences without the clutter of the old.

So where do you begin? Well, we were just talking about one bedroom closet and how it feels to "let go". Start small. Tackle one room, or even one drawer, at a time. Keep only what you love, what you use, and what truly matters. A helpful strategy is the "one-year rule" — if you haven't used it in a year, you likely don't need it. Donate, sell, or recycle these items. This clears your space, gives the stuff a second life with someone else and makes organizing what remains easier.

Organizing the items you decide to keep is equally important. If you're a Virgo you probably already do this but for the rest of us, every item should have a place, and there should be a place for every item. This simple principle creates a flow in your home that aligns with the flow you want in your life. Simply put, putting stuff in it's place reduces stress by removing the daily frustrations of misplaced items and cluttered spaces. In this transformation of your space, remember, de-cluttering and organizing create a home that is easy to clean and maintain. A space where your heart feels at ease and allows inspiration into your life.

Reflective Prompt: Take a moment to close your eyes and visualize your ideal living space. What colors, textures, and elements make you feel most at peace and energized? Make a list of small changes you can make this week to start transforming your space into your personal sanctuary.

"Big Yellow Taxi": Benefits of Nature in Your Home

Let's talk about weaving elements of nature into your living spaces, not just as decor but as partners in your journey towards a healthier, more serene life. Indoor plants are more than just pretty greenery; they are nature's air purifiers. They work silently and diligently, filtering out common toxins like benzene and formaldehyde from everyday household items. But their benefits extend beyond cleaner air; they help increase oxygen levels. Through photosynthesis, plants convert carbon dioxide into fresh oxygen, enhancing the air quality around them. They truly are nature's solar powered little air purifiers!

Imagine your home filled with lush ferns, vibrant peace lilies, and trailing ivy where each breath you take is enriched by these natural air enhancers. It's like having a forest inside your home without all the critters! Where the air is fresh making each breath deeper. Research has shown that plants in your home can decrease headaches, respiratory issues, and allergies. This greening of your space adds more than a visual appeal — it contributes to your physical well-being, making your home not just a place to live but a place to thrive.

The serenity one feels in a natural setting isn't just due to the beauty; it's deeply rooted in our physiological response to nature. Exposure to natural elements like plants and natural light significantly reduces stress and promotes a sense of tranquility. Small indoor water fountains or bamboo arrangements can enhance this effect, as these elements evoke a Zen-like atmosphere that encourages relaxation and peace. The sound of water in a small fountain can mimic the calming sounds of a babbling brook, transporting you from your living room to a tranquil forest path or a peaceful mountain stream. It's creates an environment where stress is replaced by a sense of peace and calm.

As you consider these changes, think of each plant as a breath of fresh air, each natural element a grounding touch that creates a living space that is seen and felt. It's crafting an environment where the boundaries between the indoors and the outdoors blur, where you live not just in your home but in harmony with the natural world. Let the outside in and watch as your home transforms into a living, breathing extension of the earth offering you health, peace, and beauty in every corner.

"Peace of Mind": Downsize for a Liberating Lifestyle

Downsizing is like "De-clutter and Organization" on steroids where you move from a larger place into a smaller one. Frequently, this also means relocating to a different community. Depending on what you choose to do, it can feel like a breath of fresh air. This simplification often brings profound emotional satisfaction and unexpected financial benefits. Think about it: less space means less cleaning, fewer repairs, and more savings on utilities and maintenance — leaving more money in your pocket and less on your to-do list.

Choosing the right living space as you downsize is crucial. It's not just about finding a smaller place, it's finding the right place that financially makes sense and emotionally, it feels right. Consider what matters most to you. Is it being closer to family? Having easy access to nature or cultural activities? There's something deeply comforting about curating your surroundings to reflect a more focused vision of your lifestyle. It's about quality over quantity. If you love gardening, a small yard might be important. If you despise yard work, a condo might be a better fit. The goal is to match your living environment to your needs and passions, ensuring your home supports a fulfilling lifestyle.

Ironically, downsizing can lead to having room for bigger experiences and deeper contentment. Letting go of stuff that no longer serves you and embracing a lifestyle filled with meaning, ease, and joy is on the other side of the fear that keeps us holding on. So, take that first step and consider if downsizing is a path you want to explore and start the journey toward a lighter, more unrestricted way of living that elevates your every day.

"I Lived": Invest in Experiences, Not Things

Embracing retirement with a spirit eager for adventure and meaningful experiences can transform the everyday into something extraordinary. The true richness of life isn't so much about the objects we possess but the memories we gather, the moments that make us chuckle or outright laugh when we remember them. The psychological benefits of investing in experiences rather than material possessions are vast and deep. Engaging in activities that challenge, delight, or teach you something new can boost your happiness and overall life satisfaction far more than the latest gadget ever could. As airy-fairy as this sounds, it's backed by scientific research that shows experiences enhance our sense of self and connect us more deeply, which contributes to lasting happiness.

When planning these experiences, align them with your values and interests to ensure they resonate deeply and enrich your life meaningfully. If you cherish cultural richness, consider immersing yourself in the local art scene or planning a trip to explore ancient ruins. A dance class or a hiking trip with friends could invigorate those who thrive on physical activity. Taylor these adventures to fit your unique preferences, ensuring each experience is not just a check mark in a box on a list but a cherished chapter in your life story.

The art of experiential gift-giving can also extend this philosophy beyond your own adventures. Gifting experiences, like concert tickets, a cooking class, or a weekend getaway, can offer loved ones unique joys and memories to cherish. These gifts can be more meaningful than traditional material presents because they provide an emotional experience and create bonds through shared moments. Imagine celebrating a friend's birthday not with another knick-knack for their shelves but with a day spent together at a spa or a photography workshop. These are the gifts that keep on giving long after the day is done.

Documenting these experiences is another layer of enjoyment, allowing you to relive the joy and share it with others. Creative documentation can turn memories into treasures. For example, setting up a digital photo frame in your home that cycles through photos of your adventures keeps the memories alive daily. For those who enjoy writing, capture the essence of your experiences in a journal. This preserves the experiences and allows you to reflect on them, seeing how each adventure has woven new threads into the fabric of your life.

In this lively exploration of life's potential for joy and discovery, remember, every day offers a new opportunity to create something memorable. Whether it's a quiet afternoon spent in the garden, a night out at the theater, or a trip across the country, these experiences are the pulses of excitement and joy that can define the later chapters of your story. So step out, reach out, and fill your days with experiences that bring laughter, learning, and fulfillment. Life is not a spectator sport! Jump into the fray, and make every moment count.

Take Away

As we've thoughtfully considered what makes up your home's sanctuary, harmony is the overall melody that plays. Your living space is an extension of your inner self. An environment that pleases your eye and comforts your soul. One of the most significant takeaways from our chapter is our surroundings have a profound impact on our daily experiences. Understanding this allows you to make deliberate choices, transforming your home into place where you can rejuvenate and find inspiration.

To help in understanding, I invite you to engage in a reflective exercise called "Harmony Mapping." This activity is designed to help you visualize and plan the continued evolution of your home as a harmonious haven.

Activity: Harmony Mapping Activity

Reflect on Current Spaces: Take a moment to think about each room in your home. How does each space make you feel? Which rooms uplift your spirits and which ones don't? Write these reflections down.

Identify Changes: For each room that doesn't feel right, note what changes might help. Is it the color, the furniture arrangement, or the lighting that needs tweaking? List these potential changes, however big or small they might seem.

Set Intentions: Now, turn these notes into intentions. For example, if a room feels cluttered and chaotic, your intention might be to create a more calming and organized space. Write these intentions next to each room's notes.

Create an Action Plan: Choose one room and break down the steps needed to bring your intentions to life. This might involve de-cluttering, repainting, or rearranging the furniture. Set realistic goals and timelines for these actions.

Visualize the Outcome: For each room, take a moment to visualize the end result. How will the changes impact your daily life? How will the new space make you feel? Keeping this vision in mind can be a powerful motivator as you work towards creating your harmonious home.

Review and Adjust: Harmony Mapping is not a one-time activity. As your tastes, needs, and circumstances change, so should your living environment. Make it a habit to review your Harmony Map every few months, adjusting your plans and intentions as needed to ensure your home continues to be a source of comfort and inspiration.

As we close this chapter on creating harmonious living spaces, keep in mind that your home is more than a physical place — it's an emotional and spiritual sanctuary. Every choice you make about your space, from the colors on the walls to the furniture arrangement, influences your moods, behaviors, and overall well-being. By consciously crafting these environments, you enhance your comfort and enrich your life's quality. There is additional information in Appendix A on simple steps you may want to try in the principles of Color Theory and Feng Shui in helping to create a harmonious living space.

Moving forward, the next chapter will explore the rhythms of daily routines and how crafting purposeful schedules can further enhance the quality of your retirement life. Just as we've orchestrated our spaces for harmony, we'll now tune our daily actions for fulfillment and joy, creating days that resonate with purpose and pleasure.

CHAPTER SEVEN

DEVELOP A DAILY ROUTINE WITH PURPOSE

This chapter is about creating a daily routine that is more than just a list of tasks to check off. It's about aligning your everyday actions and turning what could be mundane into something pretty damn special. Creating the perfect day for yourself isn't hard to do but, it can be daunting to start. So where to begin? Just like we've done with every previous step in this book, we start small and build on yesterday's improvements. This is the power of compound growth, similar to how compound interest grows an investment. It is so important to understand this concept that it deserves a little bit of a deeper dive into how small shifts can deliver big results over a relatively short period of time.

So why is this so important? Fair question!

Compound growth is the concept that small, incremental changes each day are added to the previous day's changes. When you do something with repeated consistently, over a short period of time it will add up to a much larger impact than you could imagine. By using the concept of compound growth we can see how daily habits can lead to significant transformations.

For example let's use walking. In this case, starting on Day 1, you walk a mile. Each day you improve your distance by 1%, meaning each day's walk is 1% longer than the previous day. At the end of thirty days your total distance will be 1.35 miles. At sixty days your distance will be 1.82 miles. At six months your total distance will be 5.27 miles!!

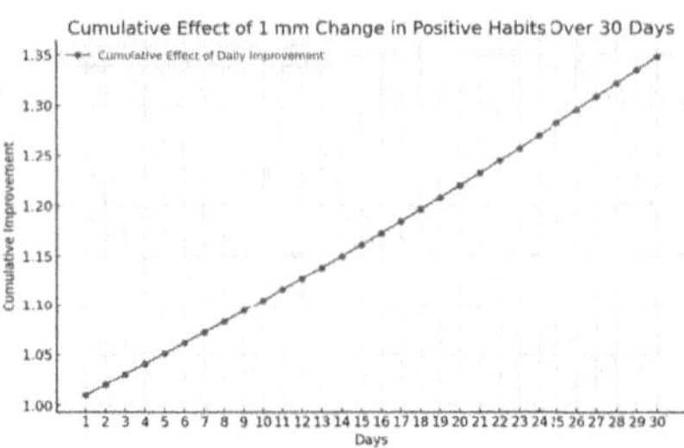

Figure 1- COMPOUND EFFECT OF 1% POSITIVE DAILY IMPROVE-MENT OVER 30 DAYS

Okay, back to a daily routine with purpose. There's a twist — the routine you create shouldn't feel like a routine! Two of my favorite mentors, Jon and Missy Butcher, created a program called "Lifebook" (available on Mindvalley) that introduced me to "sacred choices" and how to use them and create daily routines that help me move the needle forward on a physical, mental and emotional level. In a nutshell it is a structured approach to identifying what daily habits I want to consistently do to help me attain the goals in my life, one of them being writing this book! I'm not perfect and there are days when I don't check off all the boxes. But remember, this isn't about perfection, it's about progress and showing up committed to becoming the best version of yourself.

"Running on Empty": Retirement Burnout and How to Avoid It

Let's talk about "the big ugly' — burnout. We often associate burnout with the grind of a high-pressure job, but it can sneak up on you even after you retire. Yes, you read that right. Burnout in retirement is real, and more common than you might think. And, to make matters worse, you're more likely to be diagnosed as being depressed, prescribed antidepressants and patted on the head until the next existential crisis has you back in the doctor's office.

In the early days of retirement, there's a honeymoon phase: the thrill of endless free time, a break from schedules, and finally the ability to do whatever you want, whenever you want. But as time stretches out, you'll find yourself facing an unexpected reality: without structure, it's super easy to feel lost or overwhelmed and not as easy to snap out of it. Suddenly, the freedom you craved starts to feel like an empty, directionless drift. This is where burnout quietly, and often times misdiagnosed, settles in.

Retirement burnout can stem from a variety of sources — over committing to new activities, trying to fill every moment with something "productive," or feeling a sense of guilt for not living up to self-imposed expectations. You might start wondering, *"Is this all there is?"* The good news is "Hell no! This isn't all there is!" And even better is burnout isn't inevitable. It's just a signal from your mind and body that it's time to change the script. One of the most powerful antidotes is to create a daily routine of 'sacred habits' that nourish you, rather than drain you. Create your day where every action, every habit, contributes to your overall well-being. Also, know you're not alone. In fact, "I'm so tired" is one of the most frequent comments I hear from women who have just retired.

Retirement isn't a ceaseless holiday; it's a significant life transition that requires adjustment and just like any journey, it can be surprisingly draining. But here's the thing — this is perfectly normal! Think about it, after years of juggling work, family, and everything in between, your body needs time to adjust to this new phase of life. No, you won't catch up on all the sleep you've ever lost (unfortunately, there's no magical sleep bank), but cut yourself some slack and let your body rest. It's essential. Think of those naps as a well-deserved recharge not a sign of laziness. Embrace the catnaps and skip the guilt. Rest is not a luxury; it's a necessity. Remember, even the best road trips need rest stops.

The notion that retirement must be a relentless pursuit of activities is a myth that needs debunking. This idea might stem from our culture's overemphasis on productivity, where value is often measured by how busy one is. But, true fulfillment in retirement isn't about filling every moment with tasks but finding a balance that brings joy and relaxation. It's okay to have days where the most significant accomplishment is reading a novel or watching birds in the garden. These aren't wasted days! They're essential in helping you recharge and reflect.

Recharging your batteries can mean doing less or at least doing things differently. Consider your current schedule — have you packed your days with back-to-back activities to maximize your newfound freedom? While being active is wonderful, even machines need downtime. Implement what I like to call "intermezzo moments"; short, intentional breaks between activities to breathe and be. Just sitting quietly with your thoughts can be remarkably rejuvenating.

Incorporating relaxation techniques into your daily routine can also significantly help prevent burnout. Mindfulness, meditation, gentle yoga, or tai chi can lower stress levels and improve mental clarity. Consider setting aside time each day for whatever practice speaks to you. Over time, it will help you maintain your energy levels more effectively, keeping burnout at bay. Remember, retirement is a marathon, not a sprint. Pace yourself, enjoy the scenery, ensure you've got fuel in your tank and you'll be ready for whatever comes your way.

By recognizing the signs of burnout and taking proactive steps to manage your energy wisely, you ensure your retirement journey is as fulfilling and enjoyable as you envisioned. So, keep an eye on your gauges, take those refreshing pit stops, and cruise through your years with joy and vitality.

"Good Vibrations": Purpose Driven

Before diving into the specifics of building your purpose-driven routine, let's start with figuring out what 'purpose' means to you. Is it achieving specific goals? Building connections with others or making a difference in your community? Is it about personal growth? Learning something new, or simply finding joy in the everyday? Your definition of purpose will guide the structure of your routine and help you align with what's important to you.

One of the first things to consider is the natural rhythm of your day. Just like music, rhythm sets the flow of your day and you can use it to your advantage. For example, some people thrive on a fast-paced beat to a morning routine of going to the gym. Others may prefer a slower tempo, with ample space for reflection and leisure. Understanding your personal rhythm will help you design a natural and enjoyable routine that has higher likelihood of you sticking with it.

Also, keep in mind, that flexibility is critical and life is unpredictable. Most of us have spent decades in a rigid routine and it may take effort to retrain yourself. Using buffers and flexible time slots to adjust to the unexpected reduces stress. It provides you opportunities to embrace spontaneous moments of joy — those unexpected bursts of laughter, impromptu gatherings, or last-minute adventures that add a fun unpredictability to life.

With these foundational elements in place — understanding your purpose, respecting your rhythm, and allowing for flexibility — you're ready to craft a daily routine that enhances your life's melody. The stage is set, the band is ready, and it's time to live today with intention and joy.

Reflective Prompt: Reflect on your current daily routine. What activities bring you the most joy and fulfillment? What could you do more or less of to create a more purposeful and satisfying day? Write down a new morning routine that includes activities that energize and inspire you.

"Eye of the Tiger": A Rhythmic, Music-Infused Daily Ritual

Starting your day with music can be invigorating as that first cup of coffee. Consider setting up a morning wake-up playlist that acts like a gentle nudge to rise and shine. This isn't snoozing the annoying alarm clock but tunes that build gradually mirroring the sunrise. Soft instrumental pieces or acoustic favorites can coax you out of sleep with their soothing tones, setting a calm yet uplifting tone for your day. As breakfast sizzles on the stove, why not switch to something more upbeat? A playlist featuring classic hits or lively jazz can inject a dose of joy and energy into your morning routine and your first meal of the day.

Throughout the day, align your activities with the appropriate musical line-up. For instance, if you're dedicating time to physical exercise — a brisk walk, some yoga, or even gardening — curate a playlist with upbeat, energetic songs that keep your spirits high and your body moving. Music has the remarkable ability to make physical activities feel more like fun. On the flip side, opt for softer, calming tunes for moments of relaxation or tasks that require more concentration, such as reading or crafting. Instrumental music or classical pieces can wrap you in a zone of concentration, enhancing your focus and calming your mind, making intricate tasks more enjoyable and meditative.

The art of ritualizing music listening lies in creating specific times and settings where music becomes the focal point, not just background noise. Dedicate some time to just sit back, listen and actively experiencing it. Set up a cozy corner in your home with comfortable seating and good headphones. Let yourself be carried away by the songs in your playlist. Let yourself explore new music. This practice allows you to de-stress and you may notice nuances and subtleties of music's effect on you that you might miss during casual listening.

To weave music into the fabric of your daily life, maintain a journal to reflect on how different tunes influence your mood and productivity. Note which songs lift your spirits, help you concentrate, and which songs are best for relaxation. Over time, this journal will become a valuable tool, helping you make more intentional choices about your music selection and ensuring that each day is well-scored and emotionally enriched. This mindful approach to music listening encourages a deeper connection to the rhythms that underscore your daily life, enhancing each day with a soundtrack that truly resonates with your personal rhythm and mood.

By transforming music listening from a passive to an active pursuit, you enhance your enjoyment and overall well-being. The right music can transform spaces and moods, turning every part of your day into a harmonious blend of activities that are as melodious as they are meaningful. So, let the music play, let it inspire your days, and turn them into a series of joyful experiences that resonate with the rhythm of your life.

"Dream On": Start a Purpose-Driven Side Project

Discovering a side project that resonates with your soul involves a delightful exploration of your passions. Think about what excites you, what topics you read about endlessly, or what issues stir your heart. It could be anything from starting a community garden, launching a small craft business, writing a memoir, or mentoring. The key is that it should feel less like work, more like love, less like obligation, and more like exploration. Once you've pinpointed your passion, think of how this project could light up your life and the lives of others. When I first retired, I couldn't pinpoint a passion with a bazooka, so I went for things that sounded like I'd enjoy and gave myself permission to have fun exploring for answers.

Now, let's sketch the blueprint for bringing your project to life. Begin with setting clear, achievable goals. What do you hope to accomplish in three months? Six months? A year? Break these into smaller milestones. A three month goal down to monthly, then down to weekly, ending with what habits you need, daily, that move you toward your goal. These smaller milestones will act as stepping stones, marking your progress along the way. Each milestone achieved will boost your confidence and motivate you to continue. Next, consider the resources you'll need. This could involve budgeting for materials, carving out space in your home for this project, or scheduling specific times for you to work on your project. Remember, this is your symphony to compose, so arrange your resources in a way that hums with you on every level.

The ripple effects of engaging in purpose-driven work are profound. On a personal level, it can transform your retirement into a dynamic period of growth and fulfillment, keeping your mind sharp and your spirit lively. But the impact doesn't stop with you. Whether beautifying your community, preserving local history, or providing handmade gifts that bring joy to others, you can touch many lives. You are leaving a fingerprint that says, "I was here, I cared, I contributed." This legacy is a powerful component of a life well-lived, echoing your values and passions long after the project is complete.

Balancing this new passion with the other elements of your retirement life is crucial. It's like mixing a cocktail — too much of one ingredient can overpower the others. Schedule regular project times but remain flexible enough to enjoy spontaneous outings or to step back and reassess when life throws a curve ball. Take a step back if you find your project time colliding with family commitments or personal downtime. Assess what adjustments are needed to restore balance. Remember, the goal is not to add stress but to enrich your life.

Maintaining consistency in your side project is important, but strive for a rhythm that feels more like a dance than a march. For your own sake, don't berate yourself if you miss a day or a task doesn't go as planned. Instead, embrace the ebb and flow of creativity and productivity. Some days, the ideas and energy will surge like a tide; other days, not so much! This natural rhythm is part of the creative process, and learning to move with it will make your project a source of joy rather than frustration. Keep your eyes on the horizon of your goals, but allow yourself the flexibility to navigate the journey in a way that brings joy and fulfillment, not just to the destination but with every step along the way.

"Peaceful Easy Feeling": Embrace Leisure without Guilt

In your retirement, consider leisure as a vital component of your well-being. The soft, quiet moments of doing *"nothing"* outwardly can, paradoxically, add the most value to our lives. Leisure is the unsung hero in our daily lives, offering us the space to breathe, dream, and simply be. Yet, we often battle the programming from our work years and society, that whispers (or shouts) we must always be doing something to be productive. I want you to hush that annoying little voice (with or without colorful gestures) and encourage you to embrace leisure without an ounce of guilt. And, as a side effect, you'll find leisure can have a profound impact it on your health and happiness, *and thereby, the health and happiness of all around you.*

Leisure is absolutely a thing unto it's own for each of us. Maybe it's the first cup of coffee of the day being enjoyed under the infinite stars just before sunrise. Or maybe it's the quiet interest of going through a tackle box of fishing lures, or refinishing furniture, or a good book, or an afternoon walk on a nature trail. These moments don't scream productivity in any sense of the word but they are the building blocks in rejuvenating the spirit, resetting the mind, and nurturing the soul. That is the secret value of leisure, its ability to restore us, bring us back to our center, and remind us of life's simple joys.

In my opinion, the practice of "Being Leisure" is a superpower and one that can be challenging to embrace. After all, we've been trained for pretty much our entire lives that worth is tied to productivity — *our* worth is tied to *our* productivity. Breaking free from this mindset isn't as simple as snapping your fingers or clicking your ruby red slippers together. Or is it? What if what needs to change is your definition of what leisure means to you? What if you re-imagine leisure as time invested in your well-being?

So circle back to what leisure is for you, not as time wasted, but as time invested. Reflect on how different periods of leisure makes you feel. Do you notice a lightness, a freshness in your thoughts after finishing a good book? Do you find ideas flowing more freely after playing the piano or painting? Do you feel a sense of connection when you sit quietly in nature and just observe? These are the subtle yet significant benefits of leisure — signs that it's working its quiet magic on your mental and emotional health for the better.

Feeling joy is a common side effect of embracing leisure. So, as you move through your day, allow yourself these leisure moments and side effects without guilt. Let them be your sanctuary from the world's demands, a space to recharge, reflect, and revel in the joys of artfully being at leisure. Remember, leisure plays a crucial, restorative role in the art of living well — the pause between the notes, a space to recharge and reflect. Embrace these moments, and watch as they transform your days and outlook on life.

Take Away

As we create purposeful days, remember it isn't the number of things you can get done in a day, it the number of those things that mean something to you. Each thing you chose and each habit you form should align with your passions and enhance your overall well-being, creating a rhythm that is natural to you.

Reflecting on this chapter, the core takeaway is the power of intention in your daily routines. Whether it's the soul-stirring tunes that accompany your morning routine, the fulfilling progress of a passion project or the serene embrace of guilt-free leisure, each element is a deliberate choice towards crafting a day that resonates with joy and purpose. This approach not only enriches your current moments but also creates future of days that are deeply satisfying.

Activity: Daily Reflection

To integrate the insights from this chapter into your life, I encourage you to embark on the "Daily Reflection Activity." This simple yet powerful exercise is designed to help you cultivate mindfulness and intentionality in your daily routines. Here's how you can start:

Create a Reflection Journal: Choose a journal that feels personal and inviting, or create a digital document that is easily accessible. This journal will be your space to reflect on your daily experiences and insights.

End Each Day with Reflection: Dedicate a few quiet minutes each evening to reflect on your day. Write about the activities you engaged in, the music that accompanied your day, the progress on your projects, and the leisure moments. How did these experiences make you feel? Which activities brought the most joy or fulfillment?

Plan for Tomorrow: Make intentional choices for the following day based on your reflections. If a certain playlist lifted your mood, consider how you can incorporate more music into challenging parts of your day. If a project felt particularly rewarding, allocate more time to pursue it.

Track Patterns: Review your entries to identify patterns or trends. You may discover that certain types of music consistently improve your productivity or that specific projects bring you a sense of accomplishment. Use these insights to refine your routines and align them with your passions and purpose.

This activity enhances your awareness of how daily activities impact your mood and productivity. It empowers you to make ongoing adjustments that continuously improve the quality of your days. It takes proactive steps to ensure your daily life meets your needs and fulfills your desires and aspirations.

As we close this chapter, remember that each day is your playlist and you're the disc jockey. With each thing you do and each song you choose, you have the power to create a masterpiece of a day that looks beautiful and feels profoundly fulfilling. Carry this mindset forward as we transition into the next chapter, where we will explore the art of mindfulness and gratitude, further enriching life with deeper awareness and appreciation.

CHAPTER EIGHT

PRACTICE MINDFULNESS AND GRATITUDE

Mindfulness is about being fully present in the moment. It's being aware of what your thoughts are and how your body feels without passing any judgments on what you're feeling or thinking. It's very much like being a bystander watching an event. You acknowledge what the feeling and thought is but you don't react to them as you normally might be.

Gratitude is the practice of recognizing and appreciating the good things in life, big and small. It's a mindset that shifts our focus from what's lacking to what we have, fostering a sense of contentment and happiness. By acknowledging the kindness of others and the positive experiences we encounter, gratitude helps us build stronger relationships, enhances our emotional well-being, and promotes a more optimistic outlook on life. It's a simple, powerful way to cultivate joy and resilience, even in challenging times.

Cultivating a sense of mindfulness and gratitude involves weeding out the unnecessary and creating a space within yourself that welcomes peace and gratitude. Snap, right? Well, yes and no. Yes — it's a simple practice but the challenge is getting beyond a "monkey mind" that it's impossible for *you* to do because *you can't* quiet your thoughts. It's not that you don't have thoughts, you just don't hold on to them.

As mentioned one or two times already (or maybe more), starting small is less daunting and let's you explore how integrating mindfulness and gratitude into your daily life enhances your emotional well-being. Consider this powerful quote from the book **"Illusions: The Adventures of a Reluctant Messiah"**.

> "Argue for your limitations, and sure enough they're yours."
>
> Richard Bach

Stop arguing for your limitations! Stop giving energy to the very thing that's holding you back and keeping you from moving forward. Let's state the obvious. It's called a practice because you *actually* have to practice to get better at it. Incorporating a mindfulness and gratitude practice into your daily life transforms ordinary days into extraordinary ones, not because anything outside changes but because your internal perspective shifts. You start noticing the small joys and moments that often go unnoticed. This following will guide you through a simple, practical way to infuse mindfulness and gratitude into your life, making each day a little brighter and much more beautiful.

One Step at a Time: How to Start — 4 Easy Steps for Beginners

If you've ever felt like your days are slipping through your fingers, mindfulness and gratitude can slow down time and enrich every moment. Think of this as your personal life enhancer, sprinkling a little magic into your daily routines. Let's ease into this transformative practice with a few simple steps that beginners can follow easily.

- **Step 1: Start with Short, Consistent Sessions**

  Let's begin by finding a quiet corner in your home — a place where you can sit undisturbed for a few minutes each day. This could be a cozy armchair by the window or a cushion in a peaceful corner. Sit comfortably, close your eyes, and bring your attention to your breath. Breathe naturally and simply observe the flow of your breath — the way it feels coming in and going out. Your mind may wander — that's perfectly fine and normal. When you notice it drifting to chores, plans, or conversations, gently come back to your breath. This practice isn't about silencing your thoughts; it's about noticing them without judgment and returning to your breath repeatedly.

Parallel to your meditation, start a gratitude journal. Perhaps, right before you go to bed each day, jot down one or two things you're grateful for. These don't have to be grand events. Often, the small joys touch our hearts the most — the smile of a friend, a delicious meal, a beautiful sunset. The act of writing these down shifts your focus from what's lacking to what's abundant in your life, fostering a state of gratitude that can be surprisingly uplifting.

- **Step 2: Incorporate Mindfulness into Daily Activities**
Mindfulness isn't just for meditation sessions; you literally can do it anywhere and at any time. It doesn't take any special equipment either! Let's take eating as an example. At your next meal, pay attention to the experience. Turn off the TV and put down your phone; just be present with your meal. Notice the colors and smells of your food, the textures as you chew, and the flavors. Eat slowly, savoring each bite. This practice can transform a routine part of your day into a fun sensory experience. It can even help with digestion and portion control!

Another easy way to practice is mindful walking. Whether you're taking a walk in nature, strolling through a park or walking around your neighborhood, focus on the sensations of walking. The feel of your feet touching the ground, the rhythm of your steps and the air on your skin. Observe the sights and sounds around you noticing the things you would normally overlook. This can turn a simple walk into a refreshing exercise in mindfulness.

- **Step 3: Use Guided Resources**
While starting a practice on your own is commendable, sometimes, a little guidance can go a long way. This is where mindfulness apps like Headspace or Calm come into play. These platforms offer guided meditations to help you stay focused, especially in the beginning. They also provide a variety of meditations for different needs — sleep, anxiety, focus, and more — making it easier to find

something that resonates with your specific life situations. Similarly, use online resources to find gratitude prompts if you find yourself repeating the same things in your journal. These prompts can deepen your practice by helping you explore new dimensions of gratitude, keeping the practice fresh and engaging.

- **Step 4: Reflect and Adjust**

  Finally, make reflection a regular part of your practice. Once a week, take a moment to reflect on how mindfulness and gratitude are impacting your life. What changes do you notice in your stress levels, mood, or overall well-being? Are there specific practices that resonate more with you than others? Use this insight to adjust your routines. You may find that morning suits you better than evening, or writing in your gratitude journal every other day feels more natural than daily. Modify your practices to fit your lifestyle and preferences. Keeping a simple progress journal or using an app to track these reflections can provide clarity and motivation as you witness your transformation over time. Remember, the point is to use these practices to enrich your life and bring you greater peace and joy.

"The 59th Street Bridge Song (Feelin' Groovy)": Be Aware of Your Feelings and Thoughts

How do you cultivate awareness of your feelings, thoughts, and emotions while integrating gratitude and mindfulness into your everyday life? It all begins with setting small, mindful intentions each morning. Think of intentions as gentle reminders to stay present throughout your day. When you wake up, instead of rushing out of bed, take a moment to pause and set one or two mindful goals for the day. You might think, "Today, I will notice one thing that brings me joy" or "I will be aware of any opportunity to show kindness to a stranger." These small, intentional acts are powerful ways to train your brain to stay aware of the present moment.

Next, as you go about your day, practice being mindful by paying attention to your surroundings and how you feel. Whether you're washing dishes, driving, or engaging in conversation, notice the details — the temperature of the water on your skin, the texture of the steering wheel beneath your hands, or the sound of your friend's laughter. These subtle shifts in awareness help anchor you to the now, making your routine feel more meaningful without needing to drastically change anything in your life.

Gratitude, too, is most effective when paired with this heightened awareness. A simple yet powerful way to practice gratitude is by starting a gratitude jar. Each day, write down something you're grateful for, and as you place the note into the jar, take a moment to be fully aware of the feelings this gratitude evokes. Over time, watching the jar fill up becomes a tangible reminder of life's blessings, and on difficult days, revisiting those slips can help ground you in positive emotions.

Another aspect of cultivating awareness is paying close attention to your emotional state throughout the day. How do you feel when certain thoughts pop up? If you notice negative thoughts creeping in, acknowledge them without judgment. Explore what might have triggered them — become curious about your mind's patterns — but avoid clinging to them. It's about noticing, being aware, and then letting go of what no longer serves you. This process isn't about pushing away feelings or pretending everything is fine, but instead, becoming more attuned to your internal world. From this place of awareness, you can consciously choose which thoughts to keep and which to release, allowing your emotional health to flourish.

"Harvest Moon": Create a Mindful Environment at Home

In Chapter 5 we talked about creating a harmonious space in your living environment which also plays a crucial role in supporting your mindfulness and gratitude practices. Creating a space that exudes calm and positivity can significantly enhance your ability to stay centered throughout the day. A cluttered space often leads to a cluttered mind, so keeping your surroundings tidy can help maintain mental clarity.

Consider incorporating elements like a small tabletop fountain that evoke mindfulness and tranquility. Lighting is another crucial aspect. Natural light boosts mood and energy, so open those curtains and let the sunshine in. Use soft, warm lighting in darker spaces to create a peaceful ambiance. Candles are also fantastic for creating a serene atmosphere;

their gentle glow can be calming during early morning or evening hours. Of course, be the adult and don't leave your candles unattended!

Lastly, personalize your space with items that have sentimental value. Photos of loved ones, souvenirs from travels, or a crystal that you adore can serve as visual touchstones of joy and gratitude. Each time your eye catches these items they can remind you of the beautiful parts of your life, fostering feelings of contentment and thankfulness.

Integrating mindfulness and gratitude into your living environment creates a is powerful balance that enhances your overall well-being. These practices transform not only how you view the world but also how you interact with it. You encourage yourself to slow down and appreciate the abundance surrounding you, making every day a more joyful and meaningful experience. As you continue to practice mindfulness and gratitude, watch your world transform, one moment, one breath, one heartfelt minute at a time.

Reflective Prompt: Think about the current state of your home. Are there areas that feel particularly calming or chaotic? How might you de-clutter or reorganize these spaces to promote a sense of peace and mindfulness? List three small changes you can make this week to cultivate a more mindful environment at home.

"Shine On You Crazy Diamond": Craft Playlists for Relaxation

There's something almost magical about the right song at the right moment, especially when relaxation is the goal. Music can act as a powerful conduit for calm, whisking you away from the day's stresses to a more serene state of mind. Let's explore how to cultivate your musical oasis, a sanctuary of sounds that can soothe the soul, ease the mind, and gently unfurl the tightest knots of stress at the tap of your finger.

Identifying the genres that soothe you is like choosing the right ingredients for a perfect recipe. Each genre has its own flavor and impact. Just like most of us don't eat Mac and Cheese for dinner every night, sticking to the music you've always known is a good starting point but don't be shy about exploring other flavors! Classical music, with its complex harmonies and predictable progressions, can significantly lower stress levels. Of course, not everybody is into the structured beauty of Bach or the flowing melodies of Debussy.

On the other end of the spectrum is ambient music. Brian Eno, who is considered one of its pioneers, is an excellent starting place to explore this genre. Ambient music's lack of a fixed rhythm allows your brain waves to sync with the sound, leading to more profound relaxation. Nature sounds also play a pivotal role in relaxation. The crashing of ocean waves, the pitter-patter of rain, or the calming rustle of leaves can ground you in the present moment, helping your worries to ebb away with each natural note.

Crafting themed playlists is the next step in your auditory journey to relaxation. For sleep, a playlist might feature slower, softer songs that act as a gentle lullaby. Artists like Max Richter or Brian Eno have compositions that can help coax your mind into a state of restfulness. For general stress reduction, consider a mix that includes soothing acoustic tracks that comfort without demanding too much attention, allowing you to unwind as you go about your evening routines. When selecting tracks, consider their tempo, volume, and the emotions they evoke. Organizing your playlists by activity or time of day can also be helpful. For instance, creating a morning relaxation playlist with gentle but uplifting melodies can set a positive tone for the day.

Modern technology has made discovering and organizing music more accessible than ever. Music streaming services like Spotify, Apple Music, or YouTube Music offer features that can enhance your music experience. Utilize the search and recommendation features to discover new relaxation tracks. Most platforms also allow you to set up playlists for specific times, which can be particularly useful for setting up a sleep timer. You can have a playlist that gently plays for 30 minutes as you drift off to sleep, automatically turning off as you enter your night's slumber. Many streaming services offer tracks that are purely environmental sounds, or you can find apps dedicated to ambient soundscapes. Mixing these natural sounds with instrumental music can create a multi-layered auditory environment that immerses you in relaxation. For example, combining the soft sounds of a forest stream with a slow, ambient keyboard piece can transport you to a tranquil forest, all from the comfort of your living room.

Crafting these playlists of sounds are tools that help you manage stress, enhance relaxation, and improve the overall quality of your life. They are your personal retreat, a sound sanctuary where you can let go of the world's demands and tune into your inner peace.

So, take some time to explore, experiment, and create a playlist that will guide you gently along the journey of relaxation.

"Turn, Turn, Turn": Integrate Music with Meditation Practices

The art of combining music with meditation begins with selecting the right kind of music. While personal preferences certainly plays a role, there are specific types of music that naturally enhance your desired state. Ambient melodies, for instance, with their slow tempos and lack of lyrics, can help reduce mental chatter and facilitate a deeper state of relaxation. Music can support a meditative state by providing a gentle backdrop to your focused breathing or guided meditation practices.

Creating a musical meditation is just as important as the playlist. Start by choosing a space where interruptions are minimized. This could be a dedicated meditation corner with comfortable cushions and perhaps a few inspiring items like candles, crystals, or a small statue. Pay attention to the sound levels; the music should be audible but not overwhelming. Using headphones is highly recommended. Soft lighting can also help create an inviting atmosphere, making your meditation space a welcoming retreat.

Guided music meditations can serve as a bridge for those new to meditation or those looking to deepen their practice. These are meditations where a narrator guides you through meditation while music plays in the background, enhancing the experience and helping you stay focused. You can find these guided sessions on various meditation apps or online platforms. Some may use the natural cadence of classical pieces to guide your breathing, and others might use gentle acoustic melodies to help visualize peaceful landscapes. Over time, you may feel inspired to create your own guided sessions, selecting music that resonates with you and scripting meditations that address your specific needs and intentions.

As you explore different sounds and rhythms make note of the effect on your meditation and don't be afraid to experiment! Try meditating with nature sounds, like rainfall or ocean waves, and notice how they affect your sense of peace. Even instrumental tracks from various genres can offer new layers to your experience, whether it's the smooth tones of jazz or the ethereal melodies of a Enya. Your practice is uniquely yours, so let your intuition guide you in finding the sounds that resonate most deeply with you.

Remember, the beauty of combining music with meditation lies in its flexibility. Some days, a short, soothing piece might be just what you need to reset, while other times, an extended musical journey may help you unwind and reflect. There is no right or wrong way to integrate music into your practice. The intention is to enrich your meditation experience so you connect more fully with your inner calm and bring a sense of tranquility into your daily life.

"Don't Stop": Overcome Uncertainty with Uplifting Tunes

We've all have had days where the snap, crackle and pop is not coming from our bowl of rice krispies. Maybe it's the hot water heater, the dishwasher, or the termites remodeling your back bedroom. The point is there is very little in our life that would suggest we aren't capable of handling whatever comes our way. So when life throws you a curve ball, use the transformative power of music to set your emotional state like it's a super power!

So, how do you pick tunes that lift your spirits? The technical answer is start by considering the beats per minute (BPM). Songs with a higher BPM tend to feel more energetic and can naturally elevate your mood. Think of the classic hits that never fail to get people up and dancing — there's a good chance these have a faster rhythm. Lyrics also play a crucial role; opt for songs with positive, empowering messages. These can act as little affirmations sung directly to your soul, reminding you of the beauty and positivity in the world, even on a cloudy day.

Now, let's talk about creating those "mood boost" playlists. This is where you can get creative and personal. Start by gathering a list of songs that have historically made you feel happy. YouTube is a perfect starting place if you need some help getting started. Don't worry about genres or what anyone else might think — this playlist is about what makes you smile. Platforms like Spotify or Apple Music are fantastic for this, as they allow you to drag and drop songs into the order that best suits your mood trajectory.

Incorporating movement with your music listening can amplify the mood-lifting effects. Why not pair your playlist with a brisk walk or a spontaneous living room dance party of one if need be? Combining endorphins from physical activity with the dopamine released from the music is a potent mix for boosting your spirits. It's like a double shot of happiness served with a side of zest. If you're feeling adventurous, match the pace of your walk or dance to the rhythm of the music, letting the beats dictate your steps. This adds a fun challenge and deepens your connection to the music, making the experience both grounding and exhilarating.

Setting up regular therapeutic music listening sessions can also be a fantastic way to intentionally use music to improve your emotional state. Dedicate a specific time each day or week for this practice. Use good quality headphones to really immerse yourself in the sound. Close your eyes and let the music wash over you. Reflect on the emotions and memories the music evokes. This practice isn't just passive listening; it's actively engaging with the music to explore and understand your emotional landscape.

Through these strategies — selecting the right music, creating personalized playlists, combining music with movement, and setting up dedicated listening sessions — you harness the power of tunes to transform your mood and outlook on life. Music becomes more than just a series of notes and rhythms; it turns into a personal therapy session, a motivational speaker, and a loyal friend all rolled into one. So next time you feel uncertainty creeping in, remember, you have a secret weapon, just a tap or click away.

Take Away

As we lace up our shoes for our journey through mindfulness and gratitude, let us pause for a moment at the finish line of this chapter to catch our breath and reflect. The single, gleaming takeaway from our exploration is this: incorporating mindfulness and gratitude into your daily life is less about doing and more about being. It's being present in the moment, being aware of the things around you, and being kind to yourself through the ebbs and flows of emotions. This isn't just a practice; it's a way of living that makes your world happier and beautiful.

Now, let's roll up our sleeves and put these insights into practice. I'd like to introduce you to the "Mindful Moments Album," a fun and creative activity that encourages you to capture and cherish the daily instances of mindfulness and gratitude.

Activity: Mindful Moments Album

Imagine creating a scrapbook, but instead of photographs, you're collecting moments — snapshots of your day when you felt fully present or deeply grateful. Here's how you can start this enriching activity:

Gather Your Materials: Find a journal or scrapbook that resonates with you. It could be simple or ornately designed, whatever inspires you to fill its pages. Along with it, keep some pens, markers, or even some colored pencils handy.

Daily Entries: At the end of each day, take a few minutes to reflect on the moments when you were fully immersed in the present or felt a surge of gratitude. Write these instances down. Describe the sensory details: what you saw, what you heard, how you felt. This is more than capturing the moment; it's reliving it.

Decorate: Here's where your creativity kicks in. Surround your written entries with doodles, a splash of color, or a symbolic sketch. If you're crafty, you might add some mementos from the day — a leaf from your afternoon walk, a ticket stub from a movie, or a snippet of a gift wrap from a present you received.

Reflect Weekly: Once a week, flip through your entries. Notice any patterns or recurring themes. Are there certain times of the day you're more mindful? Are there specific people or activities that spark gratitude? This reflection can offer profound insights into how mindfulness and gratitude naturally weave into your life and how you might further cultivate these moments.

Share Your Journey: Occasionally, share your creation with a friend or loved family member. Discussing your experiences can deepen your understanding and may inspire others to start their own journey.

This activity reinforces mindfulness and gratitude practices and turns them into a visual and interactive art form. As you fill your journal or scrapbook, you'll notice that it becomes more than just a collection of moments — it becomes a story of your transformation, a tangible reminder of your daily growth towards a more present and thankful you.

As we close this chapter, remember that the true essence of mindfulness and gratitude lies in the practice. They are more than concepts to understand but experiences to live. Each day offers a new page, a blank canvas to consciously paint with moments of presence and appreciation. As you continue these practices, they become as natural as breathing — effortless, rhythmic, and life-sustaining. As a gift of my appreciation for you please feel free to download a free PDF version of my 21 Day Gratitude Journal using the QR code below.

CHAPTER NINE

YOUR TOOLBOX AND THE PLAYLIST OF YOUR LIFE

Welcome to the home stretch, where we fine tune the grooves and sounds that compose your, newly created, no guardrails applied, "Playlist of Life". Your playlist is an internal compass, guiding and directing you on how you perceive and interact with the world around you. You use music, or your *'one thing'*, to intentionally create a mindset that lets you take the small steps to improve whatever area of your life that you want to improve. Be it relationships, health, community, purpose, it is your choice, every day.

The only thing that can get in your way is You. Your limiting beliefs about yourself and your life are the biggest obstacles to the changes you want to make. But, because we're the fierce, unstoppable women that we are, let's shut down those nagging, self-deprecating thoughts that we all have with a prepared response. For example:

"I'm Too Old to Start Something New" — *"Age is just a number and I can begin new adventures any time I want!"*

"I Don't Have Enough Money" — *"There are many ways to enjoy a fulfilling retirement without financial stress"*

"I Dont Know Where to Start" — *"I start with small changes that build remarkable results in creating a joyful retirement."*

Side stepping self-deprecating thoughts for just a moment, consider the story about the 4-minute mile. It's the mid 1950's; modern medicine confidently adopts a belief that the human body is not capable of running a mile in under 4 minutes. But in 1954 British middle-distance runner Roger Bannister, who clearly did not adopt that belief, ran a mile in under 4 minutes. Astonishingly, a little over a month later, another distance runner ran a mile in less than 4 minutes. Months later, another and then another. These athletes were remarkable not just because of breaking the 4-minute mile barrier but because, and more importantly, they are examples of questioning limiting beliefs and inspiring others to do the same. When you live your best live you inspire others to do the same.

I'm sure at this point in our journey together you realize that these 7 steps don't have to be sequential or even in the order that I am presenting them here. There also is no requirement that you do all 7 steps. If there is only one step that resonates with you, go with it! I know without doubt that it will change your life for the better. It will also open doors to new possibilities that seem quite improbable to you at this moment in time.

In the following sections we'll go over concepts that apply to all the steps. But, before we move on, let me just say when you live your best life; being the best version of yourself ever day, the world and the people around you reap the benefits.

"Hit Me with Your Best Shot": Practice, Practice, Practice

Every great artist, athlete, and performer knows that success lies in a daily practice of becoming a 'better you' than you were yesterday. These moments are the notes of life and there's no mistaking when they're delivered with passion, precision, and practice. Your retirement is your masterpiece, a unique composition that deserves more than just a casual stroll. It's an opportunity to use your creativity, energy, and, yes, your soul, in a way that makes you happy. So, how do you lead your life with the zest it deserves?

First, recognize the power of your mindset. It will make or break your performance. A positive, proactive outlook sees opportunities and rhythm where others see obstacles and hear discord. It's the foundation of creating days infused with purpose and joy that will support you when life hits the uncomfortable and painful notes.

Second, consider the arrangement of your daily routines. Embrace that you will be making tweaks to priorities to better harmonize with your vision and dreams for your retirement. Maybe it works better for you to make appointments in the afternoon because you use the mornings to do self-care rituals of meditation and exercise, or maybe just the opposite. The point is no one but you knows what works best for you!

Whenever I consider making a tweak I run this thought program —> *"**Assess, Adjust, Activate**"*

"Do I want to do this?" ***Assess***
"If I do, what do I need to do to make it happen?" ***Adjust***
"Take action and see what happens." **Activate**

It's easier to make changes when you measure the thing you want to change and a habit tracker is a simple, yet powerful tool, to see if you are doing the things that move you towards your goal. There are many trackers available, from apps for your phone to smart watches or rings. You can also go the free, old school route and use Google Sheets . For example, when I started I tracked three targets that would improve my physical and mental well-being in a Google Sheet. Nothing fancy, if I made the target I would enter *True* and the cell turns green; if I didn't, I would enter *False* and the cell turns red. I was able to see very quickly how I was doing. I avoided being judgmental with myself and took the opportunity of seeing a red cell as a chance to re-commit to that particular target the next day. Here is a QR code to the simple 12 month tracker I use. I hope you find it useful!

Lastly, remember the power of practice and patience. Overnight sensations are exceptionally rare and most talented people spend hours practicing and perfecting their craft.

Mastering the art of a fulfilling retirement is no different — it also requires practice and patience. You continually engage with and refine your daily rituals. It's a dynamic process that grows exponentially from simple, regular reflection and adjustment of what moves the needle for you in a positive way. It isn't complicated but it does take persistence and willingness to forgive yourself when you fall short.

"Bohemian Rhapsody": Beyond the Comfort Zone

Retirement is a time of great freedom, where your schedule is yours to fill as you wish. It's also the perfect time to step outside your comfort zone. For many of us, it might be the first time we're even thinking about comfort zones. So, naturally, you might be asking yourself, "What exactly *is* a comfort zone?" A comfort zone is exactly what it sounds like; a place or situation where you are content, feel safe and are comfortable. Outside your comfort zone it's the opposite to varying degrees.

Probing your comfort zone begins with recognizing what feels familiar and comfortable — and then decide if that's where you want to push. For example, reading the morning paper each day is familiar and comfortable for you. Maybe you decide you want to start your day differently, so instead of reading the morning newspaper you get some fresh air and exercise on a morning walk listening to a podcast on a topic you know little to nothing about. While this doesn't sound like a large leap outside of a comfort zone, it actually proves the point that it doesn't have to be a large leap at all!

The place of growth is the sweet spot just beyond the edge of your comfort zone. It's where you feel slightly uncomfortable, but also excited and when done in a way that is right for you, it will expand the boundaries of your comfort zone.

A simple, step-by-step Comfort Zone Exercise:

1. **What's Your Comfort Zone:** Make a list of things that you do habitually or that feel "easy" to you. This could be routines, hobbies, or even social habits. Knowing what's comfortable is the first step toward expanding beyond it.

2. **Pinpoint the Edges**: Ask yourself what you're curious about and want to try. Is it a new hobby, volunteering, traveling solo, or joining a group? The edge of

your comfort zone is the juicy area where new adventures and possibilities begin.

3. **Take Small Steps:** Start with small actions that push your boundaries just a bit. This initial "probe" is about testing new waters, not diving headfirst into them. For example, if you're shy about meeting new people, join a local club or class related to your interests. Choose something that feels like a manageable risk.

4. **Reflect and Adjust:** After trying something new, reflect on how it made you feel. If it was slightly uncomfortable but also exciting, you're on the right track. If it was overwhelming, scale back a bit. The goal is to gradually expand your comfort zone in ways that bring excitement and growth.

5. **Build on Small Wins:** When you find an experience that, while uncomfortable, leaves you feeling accomplished or inspired, build on it. Maybe that first art class leads to joining a community group or displaying your work. The more you probe outside your comfort zone, the more those boundaries will expand.

6. **Embrace a "Playlist" Approach:** Treat this process like curating a playlist of new experiences (a theme from The Art of Retirement for Women). Some will be hits, others may not be for you, but each addition enriches your life with variety and excitement.

Exploring outside your comfort zone is less about forcing yourself into something completely new (unless that's your thing!) and more about exploring the edges of your current interests and boundaries. Find what sparks your curiosity and take one small step in that direction. It really is just that simple and the excitement of what you discover will encourage you to keep exploring!

Whether that's metal detecting, flying trick kites, volunteering, crafting, or learning a new language, each new opportunity to step out adds variety to your days, keeps your mind active and your outlook fresh. Venturing into the unknown can be exciting and a bit nerve wracking, but remember, the most rewarding experiences often lie just beyond your comfort zone. Retirement isn;t just about not working anymore — it's a time for new beginnings.

"Man in the Mirror": Live a Life That Inspires Others

Living to inspire isn't grand gestures; it's taking small, meaningful actions that can ripple through the lives of others. Simple acts of kindness — like sharing a favorite book, checking in on a neighbor, or volunteering a few hours at a local community center — can have a lasting impact. These small actions create ripples that touch others in ways you may never fully realize. And don't underestimate the power of simply listening. Sometimes, the most important thing you can do for someone is to be there, offering a compassionate ear without judgment.

Retirement gives you the time to reflect on your life and share the lessons you've learned. The stories from your experiences — whether they're about challenges you've faced, dreams you've pursued, or adventures you've had — are valuable. When you share these stories, you offer guidance and hope to others, especially younger generations. Sitting down with a grandchild or a young neighbor to share your life's journey can be more than storytelling; it can be a way to connect deeply and offer wisdom that helps them navigate their own paths.

Inspiring others isn't just about what you've done in the past; it's also about continuing to grow. Stay curious, keep learning, and try new things. Whether it's picking up a new hobby, learning a new language, or diving into a subject you've never explored before, each new skill or piece of knowledge you gain enriches your life and shows others that growth doesn't have an upward age limit. It's a reminder that life is full of opportunities, no matter where you are in your journey.

Another way to inspire is through mentorship. Consider mentoring someone who is just starting out in a career you've had, or guiding someone through life's challenges. Your insights and experience can be incredibly valuable, offering a perspective that only comes from years of lived experience. Whether it's through formal programs or informal relationships, mentoring allows you to pass on your knowledge and help shape the future.

Also, think about how you can make an impact in your community. Maybe it's advocating for a cause you care deeply about, participating in local government, or simply being a reliable volunteer, your actions can inspire others to get involved and make a difference.

These efforts don't have to be monumental — sometimes showing up consistently can have a powerful influence on those around you.

As you move forward, think of yourself as a source of guidance for others. Your experiences, wisdom, and actions can help others see the possibilities in their own lives. Live fully, love openly, and share generously. Be the kind of person who helps others find their way and inspires them to keep moving forward.

"Let It Be ": Accept the Things You Cannot Change

This may be a spoiler, but there will be moments when you realize that not everything is within your control. The art of acceptance is embracing life's changes with dignity and grace. Acceptance often starts with acknowledging the realities of life you have lived and what lies ahead. It might be the silver in your hair, the lines etched from years of laughter, or that your energy isn't what it used to be. These changes don't have to define who and it doesn't mean you have to love them. It does mean accepting them as part of your journey and shifting your focus to the present with more clarity and contentment.

Acceptance also involves letting go of long-held dreams that no longer serve you or fit your current lifestyle. This might mean moving from a family home filled with memories to something more manageable or stepping back from responsibilities that no longer bring joy. It's about recognizing when holding on is doing more harm than good and understanding that letting go can open the door to new experiences.

Finding peace in acceptance also requires tools or unique hacks that help you process and cope with change. One approach is to engage in reflective practices like journaling, where you can explore your feelings and thoughts in a safe space. Writing about your experiences allows you to process thoughts and emotions leading to a deeper understanding of the changes you're going through. Mindfulness meditation is another very helpful tool. A regular mindfulness practice can help you cultivate a sense of calm and equanimity, allowing you to face life's challenges with a more balanced perspective.

As you move forward, remember that acceptance is not about surrendering but about engaging with life in a way that prioritizes peace and well-being. Embrace each change as part of your ongoing journey and find comfort in the knowledge that every challenge also brings opportunities for growth and new experiences. Life's beauty lies in its imperfections and unexpected twists, and in accepting them, you open yourself up to the possibility of finding joy in places you never expected.

"Heroes": Being a Role Model in Retirement

The concept of heroism transcends the grandiose—it nestles in the quiet corners of everyday actions, where integrity and small deeds of kindness paint a portrait of true heroism. In the 70s, during the Cold War, David Bowie lived in Berlin. He saw a couple kissing by the Berlin Wall and saw that action as courageous. He saw two people defying the whole concept the Wall was built for; he saw them not caring about the atrocities the Wall represented. They were just kissing by it. Instead of going to a park or on the riverside, they felt like kissing by the wall. In his eyes, that made them heroes that day, inspiring his lyrics.

The true beauty of heroism in retirement, and life in general, lies in its simplicity and accessibility. You don't need to move mountains. It can be as simple as smiling at someone in the aisle at the grocery store. Think about the last time someone's act of kindness made your day — maybe someone held the door for you; maybe it was that small moment when a driver eased up on the gas, waved and let you in traffic; or maybe it was that time a neighbor brought over a meal when you were ill. These actions might seem small in the grand scheme but their impact is profound and lasting. They ripple through communities, inspiring others to pay forward the kindness they've received. This is how you can be a hero every day, positively influencing the world around you.

Encouraging you to find your heroic path involves reflecting on what matters most to you. Is it the environment, education, health, or community welfare? Once you pinpoint an area of passion, think about how you can contribute. If education interests you, perhaps you could volunteer at a local school or library, or if healthcare is close to your heart, assisting at a community health center or starting a wellness program for seniors could be your calling.

Moreover, consider the unique skills and knowledge you've amassed over the years. Your career and life experiences are invaluable; sharing this wisdom can be your heroism. Mentoring is a fantastic way to make a meaningful impact. By teaching others you enrich their lives with your wisdom and create meaningful, incredibly fulfilling connections. Picture yourself as a mentor, sharing stories of challenges you've overcome and lessons you've learned while inspiring those around to go after their dreams.

Being a role model also involves advocacy—using your voice to effect change. There are many causes and each action you take advocating for what you believe in benefits those causes and sets a powerful example for others. It shows that age is not a barrier to making a difference. Age can be an asset imbued with wisdom, experience, and a broad perspective that can drive meaningful change.

Your greatest impact might not come from grand gestures, but in the quiet moments where your presence alone gives others the courage to dream bigger. Every step you take with purpose shows the world that it's never too late to live fully and that you know, the ripples of your actions extend far beyond what you can see. Each smile, each encouraging word, each hand you lend could be the spark that lights someone else's path.

In retirement, your legacy isn't just what you leave behind—it's what you continue to create."

Take Away

As we wrap up this chapter consider this, *"each decision you make, each change you adapt to, and each day you choose to inspire or find peace enriches you beyond words in your here and now."*

Let's do a little kindness experiment together. You don't need any fancy equipment, just your lovely self and a bit of curiosity. Over the next few days, take note of how people react to simple gestures of kindness or not-so-kind.

Phase 1: Smile at people you pass by. How many smile back? How does it feel when they return the gesture? What about when someone doesn't — does it change your mood or outlook for the day?

Phase 2: Hold the door open for people as you enter or exit a building. Count how many thank yous you get. Does it surprise you how often (or how rarely) people acknowledge the gesture?

Now, here's where we flip the script.

Phase 3: Head back to the same place. This time, no smiling at strangers. Keep your facial expression neutral. What happens? Do people glance at you awkwardly or even avoid your gaze altogether? If someone holds the door for you, just walk through without saying "thank you." How does that change the dynamic? Notice how people react. Are they confused? Annoyed? Or does no one seem to care?

Phase 4: After both experiences, . Did one behavior (kindness or indifference) feel more fulfilling than the other? How did people respond? What does this tell you about the power of small, everyday acts of kindness on other people? What does this show you about the power of small, everyday acts of kindness on yourself?

As we come to the end of this chapter, know that the playlist of your life is far from complete. Each day, you get to add new songs, new experiences, and new rhythms. Some days will be slow ballads, others upbeat anthems — *either way, you're in control of the playlist*. Embrace the changes, dance through the challenges, and don't be afraid to hit repeat on the moments that bring you joy. Retirement is your time to live boldly, rewrite the rules, and let your life's soundtrack play louder than ever. You've earned this encore, so go out there and make it legendary.

CONCLUSION

Well, here we are at the end of this book — one I hope felt more like a good chat over coffee instead of a lecture. We've laughed, we've reflected, and maybe we've even thought, *"Why didn't someone tell me this 20 years ago?"* Retirement is supposed to be a reward for all those years of work, right? Yet it's funny how it shows up like an uninvited houseguest, with too much time on its hands and no idea where to sit. It's not always the golden moments we imagined — more like slightly tarnished silver at first.

You've spent your life being everything to everyone — now it's time to be something for yourself. Maybe it's learning how to line dance, or finally reading War and Peace, or simply figuring out how to fix your printer without calling your children, the important thing is that you keep moving forward. But — and there's always one — keep this mind:

1. **There's No Such Thing as a "Perfect" Retirement:** Let's get this out of the way: some days, you'll feel like you've nailed this retirement thing. You'll be sipping tea, looking out over your flourishing garden, thinking, *"I've mastered life."* Other days, you'll wonder about the exact opposite. That's normal. Embrace the mess, the awkward starts, and the occasional *"What on earth am I doing?"* moments. Some of the best memories come from the unexpected.

2. **Learn to Laugh at Yourself:** If you ever find yourself panicking because you can't remember why you walked into a room or why your grocery list has "mail the cat" on it, take a breath and laugh. Life is too short for anything else. Humor is your greatest ally — it turns the mundane into an adventure, and the mishaps into stories you'll tell again and again. There's power in laughing at the absurdity

of life, especially when you're trying to figure out your next move.

3. **Rediscover What You Love — and Who You Love:** Remember, retirement isn't just about finding more time for yourself — it's a chance to surround yourself with the people and passions that make you feel alive. It's your turn. Make time for the things that truly matter — whether that's a hobby you lost along the way or a conversation with a friend who knows you better than you know yourself. At the end of the day, it's not the big events that shape our lives, it's the people and little joys that fill the spaces in between.

If I were to summarize this entire book into one paragraph it would be this — the days ahead, like those already lived, will come with its share of ups, downs, and in-betweens. You'll have days where you think you've figured it out, and days where you'd rather just stay in bed and watch reruns. And guess what? That's perfectly fine. Retirement isn't a destination to arrive at, it's a journey, and every step, every stumble, every leap — is part of the adventure. There's no roadmap for this, and that's the beauty of it. You've earned the right to color outside the lines, to change the script whenever you like, to wear two different colored socks and to decide, maybe for the first time, what you want to do *just for you.*

As you stand at the crossroads of what has been and what is yet to come, let this moment be a celebration of you — the woman who has dared to imagine her retirement as a masterpiece, an encore, and a time to thrive. You've walked through this book, gathering tools, ideas, and inspiration. Now, it's time to take the stage of this new chapter, not with hesitation but with the boldness of someone who knows the best is yet to come.

Take a moment to pause and reflect on the ideas we've explored together. You've rediscovered the importance of passion and how it fuels the soul. You've been reminded that your health — both physical and mental — is the rhythm that keeps the symphony of your life harmonious. You've recognized the unparalleled joy of connections, both old and new, and the beauty of a mind that never stops learning. And perhaps most importantly, you've embraced the power of mindfulness and purpose in crafting days that feel deeply meaningful.

What will you do next? Retirement is your blank canvas, waiting for the strokes of your unique creativity. Maybe it's finally diving into that long-forgotten passion project, reaching out to an old friend, or simply learning to embrace the quiet joys of a morning cup of coffee with gratitude. Whatever it is, let it be something that sparks joy and brings a smile to your face. This is your time. There are no rules about what it has to look like. Take chances. Follow an idea you had 30 years ago. Let yourself indulge in the joy of discovery, of trying new things, of failing spectacularly and laughing when you do. The truth is, there's no right way to retire — there's only *your* way. And in the end, when you look back, I hope you can say you used every ounce of joy, every talent, every moment of silliness, and left nothing on the table.

As someone who once stood where you are now, I can promise you this: the magic lies in the doing. Retirement isn't about having all the answers — it's about embracing the questions and savoring the adventure of finding what lights you up. And remember, it's okay to stumble, to change your mind, or to try again. The only rule is to keep going, one beautifully imperfect step at a time.

And as you carve out this path for yourself, consider the ripple effects. The choices you make now — whether to be bold, curious, or compassionate — create a legacy that touches those around you. Perhaps it's the courage you show in learning something new that inspires your grandchildren or the joy you find in small things that encourages a friend to rethink what's possible for them. Retirement is not a solo endeavor; it's a gift that enriches not only your life but also the lives of those who share it with you.

If you take nothing else from these pages, let it be this: the encore is yours to craft. Fill it with music that makes your heart sing, relationships that nurture your soul, and moments that remind you of the sheer wonder of being alive. Play it loud. Dance if you feel like it. Rest when you need to. Above all, remember — as Bon Jovi so rightly put it, *"It's your life—it's now or never!"*

Now, take a deep breath, and go create a life that feels as good as it looks. Retirement isn't the end of the story; it's your standing ovation. Bravo.

***

I would love to hear your journey into and through retirement. Connect with me via email me using the QR code below. Your feedback will help me improve my work to better serve readers like you.

A FAVOR BEFORE YOU GO? REVIEW REQUEST — KEEPING THE SPIRIT ALIVE

Well, my dear reader, it is my heartfelt hope that there was at least one moment in this book that made you chuckle or at least provided you with one big idea on what may be next for you. If you have enjoyed this book, I need a favor. Would you pass on your newfound knowledge and show other readers where they can find the same help by leaving a review?

Simply by leaving your honest opinion of this book on Amazon, you'll show other women where they can find the inspiration and passion for a fulfilling retirement.

Click here to leave your review on Amazon.

Thank you from the bottom of my heart for allowing me to join your journey. The joy and spirit of retirement are kept alive when we pass on our knowledge and experience. I appreciate you're helping me to do just that.

I hope you feel inspired to live your moments ahead with the vibrant emotions of love, kindness, curiosity, and joy. Connect with me on my email. I would love to hear how your "one thing" shapes your journey into and through retirement. Your stories are the melodies that can inspire others, and your feedback will help me tune my work to better serve readers like you.

Here's to *your* "Playlist for Life". Keep grooving, growing, and, above all, playing those tunes that keep you smiling through life.

Your biggest fan,
Barbara J. de Eduardo

REFERENCES

9 Virtual reality tours you'll love - Google Arts & Culture. (n.d.). Google Arts & Culture. https://artsandculture.google.com/story/mwJiZHf_Y7FfLg

20 Ways John Lennon Changed the world. (n.d.).Mojo. https://www.mojo4music .com/articles/the-mojo-list/20-ways john lennon-changed-the-world/

AARP. (n.d.). *9 Health benefits of music as you age,stress relief, improved mood among top perks cited by older adults, AARP-backedpoll finds.* https://www.aarp.o rg/health/conditions-treatments/info-2024/health-benefits-of-music.html

Admin, & Admin. (2023, July 4). Embracing Minimalism: A guide to Simplify your lifestyle. *Vicc 4 Life.* http://www.vicc4life.com/embracing-minimalism-a-guide-to -simplify-your-lifestyle/

Admin, L. (n.d.). *Unlocking Secrets: How the lazy stay motivated to exercise.* The Lazy Site. https://thelazysite.com/fitness/how-the-lazy-stay-motivated-to-exercise/

Cohn, P., & Cohn, P. (2024, January 22). *Sports Visualization for Athletes | Sports Psychology Tips.* Sports Psychology Tips| Sport Psychology Articles for Athletes, Coaches, and Sports Parents. https://www.peaksports.com/sports-psychology-b log/sports-visualization-athletes/

Community Engagement Strategies for Isolated Seniors. (n.d.). https://www.nautilusshc.com/blog/community-engagement-for-seniors#:~:text=Exam

ples%20of%20successful%20community%20engagement,share%20similar%20interests%20and%20experiences

Elevating Growth: Lifelong learning initiatives unleashed. (2024, January 29), https://resumelanguage.net/elevating-growth-lifelong-learning-initiatives-unleashed/

Corinne. (2022, August 4). *5 places every beginning musician should perform.* Promolta Blog. https://blog.promolta.com/places-beginning-musician-perform

Emling, S. (2017, December 7). Introducing 50 people who've reinvented themselves after 50. *HuffPost.* https://www.huffpost.com/entry/50-over-50_n_5635490

Evans, S., & Evans, S. (2023, December 16). How to Deal with Retirement Anxiety. *Self Help Education.* https://selfhelp.education.com/financial-self-care/retirement-planning/how-to-deal-with-retirement-anxiety/

Faith, & Faith. (2021, January 4). How to combine mindfulness and music therapy - Sound Well Music Therapy, PLLC. *Sound Well Music Therapy, PLLC - Create Sound Well-Being Through Music.* https://soundwellmusictherapy.com/combining-mindfulness-and-music-therapy/

Flynn, S. (2022, February 11). *Where to find the best online detective forums (and help solve real crimes).* Lifehacker. https://lifehacker.com/where-to-find-the-best-online-detective-forums-and-hel-1848510310

Health benefits of indoor plants. (n.d.). https://www.piedmont.org/living-real-change/health-benefits-of-indoor-plants

Hello Im 50ish. (2023, January 12). *The Ultimate Self-Care Guide for women over 50.* Hello I'm 50ish. https://helloim50ish.com/the-ultimate-self-care-guide-for-women-over-50/

Houseplants: to support human health / RHS. (n.d.). Royal Horticultural Society. https://www.rhs.org.uk/plants/types/houseplants/for-human-health

How Aging Adults Benefit from Music | Banner Health.(n.d.)
. https://www.bannerhealth.com/healthcareblog/teach-me/the-benefits-of-musi
c-on-the-mind-and-body-of-older-adults

How to be happier Regardless of your situation: Dr Michael Vivian – Suck City. (n.d
.). https://www.futurenetworkstrinity.net/how-to-be-happier-regardless-of-your
-situation-dr-michael-vivian/

Creating a musical 'Scrapbook.' Interlude HK Limited. (2019, August 29). https:
//interlude.hk/creating-musical-scrapbook/

IQ Newswire. (2023, December 28). Painting Paradise:Creating your dream home,
one stroke at a time - VyvyMangas. *VyvyMangas.* https://www.vyvymangas.com/
painting-paradise-creating-your-dream-home-one-stroke-at-a-time/

Isabel Gloria. (2022, July 21). *Shattering Stereotypes: How Today's Women Over 50
are Redefining What's Possible On-screen, at Work, and at Home.* Nielsen.
https://www.nielsen.com/insights/2021/shattering-stereotypes-how-todays-wome
n-over-50-are-redefining-whats-possible-on-screen-at-work-and-at-home/

Jackson, F. (2020, October 8). Breathe Easy With These Air-Purifying Plants.
AllPlants. https://allplants.com/blog/lifestyle/breathe-easy-with-air-purifying-h
ouse-plants

Johnson, C. (n.d.). *25 Tips to Stay Safe as a Solo Female Traveler. Showit Blog.*
Retrieved August 28, 2024, from https://heyciara.com/safesolofemaletravel/

Julian, J. (2023, August 2). Bruce Springsteen's effective fitness tip for staying cut
after 70. *Medium.* https://medium.com/famously-healthy/bruce-springsteens-1
-effective-fitness-tip-for-staying-cut-after-70-50bd9c33d287

Keep Your Brain Young with Music. (2022, April13). Johns Hopkins Medicine. https://www.hopkinsmedicine.org/health/wellness-and-prevention/keep-y
our-brain-young-with-music

Langhammer, B., Bergland, A., & Rydwik, E.(2018a). The Importance of Physical Activity Exercise among Older People. *BioMed Research International, 2018*, 1–3. https://doi.org/10.1155/2018/7856823

Lifestyle, S. (2021, December 6). 40 Mental Health Resources for Seniors | Senior Lifestyle. *Senior Lifestyle.* https://www.seniorlifestyle.com/resources/blog/40-m ental-health-resources-for-seniors/

Making friends after 50. (2024, March 6).WebMD. https://www.webmd.com/he althy-aging/making-friends-after-50

McMullen, C. (2021, October 25). *Best VR space experiences.* Space.com. https:// www.space.com/best-vr-space-experiences

Meister, S. (2023, September 25). *15 Feng shui principles to follow in your home to feel less stressed & more grounded.* PureWow. https://www.purewow.com/home/f eng-shui-basic-guide

Mfa, R. J. S. (2020, November 10). *10 ways that singing benefits your health.* Health-line. https://www.healthline.com/health/benefits-of-singing

Mooses Valley. (2021, May 28). *City Slickers 1991 -Curly's The Secret of Life - The ONE Thing (Jack Palance and Billy Crystal)*[Video]. YouTube. https://www.yout ube.com/watch?v=A2mYlZzo4cM

MSEd, K. C. (2024, February 20). *Color psychology:Does it affect how you feel?* Verywell Mind. https://www.verywellmind.com/color-psychology-2795824

Muezza, & Muezza. (2024, January 11). Stream lined living: De-clutter and organize your space. *castlemanager - Home & Garden.* https://castlemanager.net/streamli ned-living-declutter-and-organize-your-space.html

Nanou, E. (2020, December 22). *6 best VR travel apps to explore the world with your smartphone.* MUO. https://www.makeuseof.com/best-vr-travel-apps-android-ip hone/

News-Medical. (2023, September 11). *Hobbies protect older people from age-related decline in mental health and well-being.* https://www.news-medical.net/news/20230911/Hobbies-protect-older-people-from-age-related-decline-in-mental-health-and-wellbeing.aspx

Nishan. (2023, July 16). *Frugal Living: Embracing a minimalistic approach to personal finances.* https://nishankhatri.xyz/frugal-living-embracing-a-minimalistic-approach-to-personal-finances/

Pensky, C. (2024, February 19). *Benefits of music therapy for the elderly.* Miami Jewish Health. https://www.miamijewishhealth.org/blog/senior-health-wellness/benefits-of-music-therapy-for-the-elderly/

Qorbani, S., Majdabadi, Z. A., Nikpeyma, N., Haghani,S., Shahrestanaki, S. K., & Poortaghi, S. (2024). The effect of participation in support groups on retirement syndrome in older adults. *BMCGeriatrics, 24*(1). https://doi.org/10.1186/s12877-024-04923-4

Samantha Brown. (2017, December 5). *How to make the ultimate road trip playlist.* Samantha Brown's Places to Love. https://samantha-brown.com/ideas/creating-road-trip-playlist/

Virtual tour. (n.d.). Smithsonian National Museum of Natural History. https://naturalhistory.si.edu/visit/virtual-tour

Wellness, A. (2021, August 9). *Tips for creating playlists for sleep and relaxation.* Aquarius Wellness. https://aquariuswellness.com/tips-for-creating-playlists-for-sleep-and-relaxation/

Why Empathy is the Key to Success. (n.d.). http://www.reshyldelpilar.com/2023/02/why-empathy-is-key-to-success.html

Wikipedia contributors. (2024, May 3). *Social effects of rock music.* Wikipedia. https://en.wikipedia.org/wiki/Social_effects_of_rock_music

Appendices

Appendix A – Practical Steps to Get Started with Virtual Reality

To set up a virtual reality (VR) system, you'll need several components. Here's a breakdown of what you'll need:

1.   VR Headset: The VR headset is the core of any VR system. Some popular options include:

- Meta Quest 2: A standalone headset that doesn't require a PC

- Valve Index: Known for high-quality visuals and precise tracking, but requires a PC

- PlayStation VR2: Works with the PlayStation 5 console

- HTC Vive Pro 2: A high-end PC VR headset

2.   Compatible Computer or Console

- For headsets like Valve Index and HTC Vive Pro 2 you will need a computer. Ensure your PC meets the required specifications (usually a high-end CPU, GPU, and sufficient RAM)

- Gaming Console: For PlayStation VR2, you'll need a PlayStation 5

3.   VR Controllers

- Most VR packages come with controllers that allow you to interact with the virtual environment. These are typically included with the head set but verify to be sure

4.   Tracking Sensors (if required)

Some VR systems use external sensors for tracking movement, while others use inside-out tracking built into the headset

Valve Index: Requires external base stations

Meta Quest 2 and HTC Vive Pro 2: Use inside-out tracking

5.   Accessories (Optional)

- VR Ready Headphones: For immersive audio

- Cable Management Systems: For tethered headsets,to manage cables

- Comfort Accessories: Replacement face pads, VR covers, etc

- Room Setup: Ensure you have a safe, clear space to move around

6.   Software

- VR Games and Applications: Available on platforms like SteamVR, Oculus Store, and PlayStation Store

- VR Software: Ensure you have the necessary software installed on your PC or console to run the VR system

Example Setups

Standalone Setup (e.g., MetaQuest 2)

- Meta Quest 2 headset and controllers

- Optional accessories: VR cover, carrying case

PC VR Setup (e.g., Valve Index)

- Valve Index headset, controllers, and basestations

- VR Ready PC

- SteamVR software

Console VR Setup (e.g.,PlayStation VR2)

- PlayStation VR2 headset and controllers

- PlayStation 5 console

- PlayStation VR software

Ensure you check the specific requirements and compatibility for the VR system you choose.

Appendix B

Practical Steps to Get Started Creating a Harmonious Living Space

- **Start with a Vision Board:** Gather images, colors, and textures that inspire you and represent your ideal space. This can be a physical board with magazine cutouts or a digital one on platforms like Pinterest. Use it as a guide to keep your vision focused.

- **De-clutter Ruthlessly:** Begin by clearing out items that no longer serve you or bring you joy. Tackle one small area at a time, such as a drawer or a shelf. This not only frees up physical space but also creates mental clarity.

- **Choose a Focal Point:** In each room, decide on a focal point that draws the eye and sets the tone. It could be a piece of artwork, a beautiful piece of furniture, or a window with a great view. Arrange your furnishings to highlight this feature.

- **Incorporate Personal Touches:** Add elements that reflect your personality and experiences. Family photos, travel souvenirs, and handmade crafts can make your space feel uniquely yours. Remember, it's these personal touches that turn a house into a home.

- **Play with Color and Light:** Experiment with different colors and lighting to create the mood you desire. Soft, warm lights can make a space feel cozy, while bright, natural light can make it feel airy and open. Don't be afraid to try bold colors if they make you happy.

- **Invest in Comfort:** Ensure that your home is not only beautiful but also comfortable. Invest in quality seating, cozy blankets, and soft pillows. Your home should be a place where you can relax and unwind.

- **Maintain and Evolve:** Keep your space tidy and make adjustments as needed. Your home should evolve with you. Regularly reassess and tweak your décor to ensure it continues to meet your needs and preferences.

Color Psychology Tips on the Right Color Scheme for Harmony

Embrace Warm Colors for Energy and Welcome:

- Imagine a room bathed in the warm hues of a sunset. Reds, oranges, and yellows bring energy, warmth, and a sense of welcome. Think of a dining room with terracotta walls that make every meal feel like a cozy gathering by the fire.

- **Pro Tip:** Use these colors strategically. Balance them with neutral tones or use them in smaller doses to avoid overwhelming your senses.

Dive into Cool Colors for Calm and Relaxation:

- Blues, greens, and purples are your go-to for creating a tranquil space. A bedroom in soft blue can remind you of a clear sky, while sage green tiles in a bathroom can echo the serene outdoors.

- **Pro Tip:** Pair these cool colors with soft textures and subtle lighting to enhance the relaxing vibe.

Use Light Colors to Create the Illusion of Space:

- Light colors like cream, beige, and pale gray can make a room feel larger and more open by reflecting light. Perfect for smaller rooms or areas with limited natural light.

- **Pro Tip:** Transform a small kitchen with soft ivory cabinets to turn a cramped space into a welcoming nook.

Dark Colors for Cozy Intimacy:

- Dark colors such as navy or charcoal can make larger rooms feel cozier and more intimate. Think of a deep green alcove in a large living room, perfect for curling up with a book.

- **Pro Tip:** Use dark colors in bigger spaces to create a grounded and secure atmosphere.

Master the Art of Complementary Colors:

- Complementary colors, found opposite each other on the color wheel, enhance each other's vibrancy. Imagine a room with soft gray walls and vibrant blue and orange accents.

- **Pro Tip:** Mix and match complementary colors to add dynamic visual interest without clashing.

Balance and Layering for True Harmony:

- Achieving harmony involves more than picking your favorite shades. It's about creating balance and layering colors in a way that reflects your personality and supports your well-being.

- **Pro Tip:** Start with a neutral backdrop and layer in colors that make you happy through cushions, curtains, and artwork.

Final Step: Make It Your Own

- Incorporating elements of color psychology into your home doesn't require a radical overhaul. A few touches here, a splash of paint there, and you can entirely shift the mood and perception of your space.

- Think of it as creating your perfect playlist, with each color adding its own unique beat to your home's harmony. So grab those paint swatches, let your personality shine through, and remember: your home is your canvas. Paint it in colors that bring you joy, comfort, and beauty. And if anyone asks why your living room is the color of a Tuscan sunset, just tell them it makes your soul sing.

Feng Shui Fundamentals: Optimize Flow, Balance, and Energy Within a Space

Clear the Pathways:

- Think of your home as a flowing river of energy. The walkways should allow for easy, unobstructed movement, promoting physical ease and letting the energy, or 'Chi', circulate freely.

- **Pro Tip:** Walk through each room and notice any furniture blocking the flow. Rearrange pieces to clear the pathways and create a dance floor where energy can waltz freely.

Balance and Symmetry:

- Balance and symmetry play a crucial role in Feng Shui. Placing furniture in pairs or symmetrical arrangements can promote harmony within the space.

- **Pro Tip:** Think of the symmetry of a butterfly's wings. Arrange two identical armchairs facing each other for positive social exchanges or symmetrical nightstands flanking your bed for restful sleep.

The Commanding Position:

- Position key pieces of furniture, like your bed or desk, in a spot that allows you to see the door without being directly in line with it. This promotes a sense of control and security.

- **Pro Tip:** In your bedroom, place the bed so you can see the door without your feet facing it directly. This reduces subconscious stress and promotes restful sleep.

Incorporate Natural Elements:

- Bringing elements of nature into your home enhances the flow of positive energy. Use plants, water features, and natural materials to create a serene environment.

- **Pro Tip:** Add a small indoor fountain or a few potted plants to promote tranquility and connect with nature.

Use Color Wisely:

Colors influence the energy of your space. Use the psychology of colors to enhance different areas of your home. For example, use calming blues and greens in the bedroom and energizing reds and yellows in social spaces.

Pro Tip: Choose colors that resonate with the function of each room, enhancing both the aesthetic and the energy flow.

De-clutter and Organize:

- A clutter-free space allows energy to flow more freely. Keep your home organized and only hold onto items that serve a purpose or bring joy.

- **Pro Tip:** Regularly assess your space and de-clutter to maintain a harmonious environment. Every item should have a place, and every place should have an item.

Personalize with Meaningful Décor:

- Decorate with items that hold personal significance and positive energy. This adds a unique touch and reinforces a positive atmosphere.

- **Pro Tip:** Use family photos, cherished mementos, and meaningful art pieces to personalize your space andenhance its positive energy.

Final Step: Incorporating Feng Shui principles doesn't require a major overhaul of your home

- it's about making thoughtful adjustments that enhance the flow, balance, and energy of your space. By arranging your space to promote good energy flow, balance,and commanding positions, you're not just decorating; you're inviting positivity, tranquility, and well-being into your life.

- So, take a moment to assess your space, make the necessary tweaks, and transform your home into a Shambala, a haven of peace and happiness, where every corner resonates with good Chi and every room invites you to live your best, most balanced life. And remember, if anyone asks why you're rearranging your furniture, just tell them you're getting your Chi together!

Appendix C

How to Use Daily Music Reflection Journal

- Start your day with a wake-up song that gently coaxes you out of sleep, then move on to a more upbeat tune for breakfast to set a joyful tone for the morning.

- As you go about your daily activities, choose energetic tracks for exercise and softer, instrumental pieces for tasks requiring concentration. In the evening, wind down with calming music, reflecting on how each song influenced your mood and productivity.

- Over time, this journal will help you curate the perfect soundtrack for your life, enhancing each day with the power of music.

Daily Music Reflection Journal

Date: ______________

Wake-Up Song:

- Title: ____

- Artist: ____

- Mood: ____
  [how did it made you feel?]

Breakfast Song:

- Title: ____

- Artist: ____

- Mood: ____
  [how did it influence your morning?]

Movement (Exercise) Playlist:

- Movement: _____________________________________

- Title: ____

- Artist: ____

- Energy Level: __________________________________
  [how did it influence your relaxation and mood?]

Concentration/Focus:

- Title: ____

- Artist: ____

- Focus Level: _______________________________

  [how did it influence your productivity?]

Relaxation/Reading Playlist:

- Title: _______________________________

- Artist: _______________________________

- Relax Level: _______________________________

  [how did it influence your relaxation and mood?]

Evening Ritual:

- Title: _______________________________

- Artist: _______________________________

- Relax Level: _______________________________

  [how did it influence your relaxation and mood?]

Wind-Down Song:

- Title: _______________________________

- Artist: _______________________________

- Chill Level: _______________________________

  [how does it helps you unwind?]

Overall Reflections:

- _______________________________

- _______________________________

- _______________________________

- _______________________________

Daily Reflection Journal

How to Use This Journal Page:

- **Morning Reflection:** At the start of your day, note down planned activities, the music you intend to play, and any initial feelings or insights.

- **Midday Reflection:** Halfway through your day, jot down what you've done so far, the music you've listened to, and how it's all made you feel.

- **Evening Reflection:** At the end of the day, reflect on the day's activities, the music that accompanied you, and your overall feelings and insights.

- **Alignment with Values:** Assess which activities aligned with your values and which ones didn't. Identify meaningful activities and energy drainers.

- **Plan for Tomorrow:** Based on your reflections, make intentional choices for the next day. Choose music that uplifted your mood and plan projects that brought you joy.

- **Patterns &Trends:** Track recurring patterns that improve your productivity and mood. Use these insights to continuously refine your daily routines.

By regularly using this journal, you'll enhance your awareness of how daily activities impact your mood and productivity, making proactive adjustments to improve the quality of your days. It's about creating a daily life that meets your needs and fulfills your desires and aspirations.

Daily Reflection Journal

Date: _______________

Morning Reflection:

Activities:

- ____

Music:

- ____

Feelings & Insights:

- ____

Midday Reflection:

- ____

  - Activities:

- ____

Music:

- ____

Feelings & Insights:

- ____

Evening Reflection:

- ____

Activities:

- ____

Music:

- ____

Feelings & Insights:

- ____

Alignment with Values:

- ____

  - Meaningful Activities:

- ____

Energy Drainers:

- ____

Plan for Tomorrow:

- ____

Intentional Choices:

- ____

Music to Incorporate:

- ____

Projects to Pursue:

- ____

Patterns & Trends:

- ____

Consistent Mood Lifters:

- ____

Productivity Boosters:

- ____

Accomplishing Projects:

- ____

Daily Gratitude Journal Page

What am I grateful for?

How do I feel?